"The best busines... **basics again and again. This book is about some basics. Don't be deceived by its simple appearance; HUMAN BE-ING is a classic."**

—**James A. Vaughan, Ph.D.
Corporate consultant and
co-author of *Training in Industry***

- How to break through the power struggle between two people, whether they are mates, family, friends or coworkers.

- How to accept your emotions, good or bad, instead of letting others define how you should feel.

- How learning to love yourself frees you to love others.

- How to communicate effectively, and to listen to what others have to say.

Here at last is a guide that lets you almost instantly identify your problems and see how to solve them. Here is a work of insight and understanding that will begin to help you from the opening pages to its final chapter.

DR. WILLIAM V. PIETSCH is a consultant, writer and lecturer on human relationships. He is a graduate of Northwestern University and Princeton Theological Seminary, and completed a three-year residency at the American Foundation of Religion and Psychiatry in New York. He has appeared on numerous radio and television programs. Currently, he is working on a book about science, psychology and religion.

Human BE-ing

HOW TO HAVE A CREATIVE RELATIONSHIP INSTEAD OF A POWER STRUGGLE

Written and Illustrated by
WILLIAM V. PIETSCH

Foreword by George C. O'Neill

A SIGNET BOOK

NEW AMERICAN LIBRARY

SIGNET TRADEMARK REG. U.S. PAT. OFF. AND FOREIGN COUNTRIES
REGISTERED TRADEMARK—MARCA REGISTRADA
HECHO EN WINNIPEG, CANADA

SIGNET, SIGNET CLASSIC, MENTOR, ONYX, PLUME, MERIDIAN AND
NAL BOOKS are published by NAL PENGUIN INC.,
1633 Broadway, New York, New York 10019

FIRST SIGNET PRINTING, JULY, 1975

9   10   11   12   13   14   15   16

PRINTED IN CANADA

To Mike
who had faith in
my be-ing

TABLE OF CONTENTS

FOREWORD by George C. O'Neill   **9**

INTRODUCTION   **15**
The problem of power   16
Seeing the expected   20

CHAPTER I
TRANSFERENCE AND POWER STRUGGLES   23
Transference defined   25
Transference in power struggles   31
Origins of transference   35
Origins of power struggles   41

CHAPTER II
THE ORGANIC NATURE OF HUMAN BEINGS   50
The growth process   53
When growth is hindered   57

CHAPTER III
PROVIDING CONDITIONS FOR BE-ING   65
The need to BE   68
Pressure on BE-ing   70
Release of pressure   74

CHAPTER IV
TRUSTING, LISTENING, AND CLARIFYING   78
Trusting   79
Listening   89
Clarifying   98
Summary   133

CHAPTER V
HAVING THE COURAGE TO BE   136
    Love for self   137
    "Self" territory   141
    Defining territory and the "Ouch!" line   146
    Reclaiming Territory   147
    "Advice" and "Information"   152
    Summary   164

CHAPTER VI
EXPLORING ALTERNATIVES   168
    "Meaning" in relationships   170
    Looking at the problem   171
    Exchanging information   174
    Check list   181
    Summary   182

AFTERWORD
RISKING CHANGE   185
    Seeing ourselves   187
    Letting others see us   190
    Effect of risk on relationships   194

Appendix A
    Summary Example 1. IN A HOME   203
    Summary Example 2. AT WORK   217
    Comments on the process   231

Appendix B
    Comments on the check list   235

Bibliography   253

PREFACE

This book has come out of life experiences, beginning in 1954, with a workshop in counseling in Harper Hospital in Detroit, with the Rev. Malcolm Ballinger, and later in 1962, clinical training in The Ohio State University Hospital under the supervision of the Rev. Maurice Clark.

The influence of these two people led to further training in the residency program at the American Foundation of Religion and Psychiatry* in New York, beginning in 1965. I am indebted to many on the extremely capable faculty there, especially to Richard L. Johnson, M.D., Wilbert R. Sykes, M.D. and the Rev. Clifford McLaughlan for their teaching, supervision, and thoughtful insights.

Without the personal trust of those who came to me for counseling, this book could not have been written. Through their sharing, and together facing practical problems which had no easy answers, I have found a new meaning in the word "religious," and a new respect for the power of the human spirit.

An invitation to provide a lecture series for the Congregational Church of New Canaan, Connecticut provided an impetus to think through the structure of this material. This is not a "religious" book in the usual sense of the

*Renamed The Institutes of Religion and Health 1972

word, however. It is left to the reader to relate
what is said here to his own religious
perspective.

In the preparation of the book itself, I am
grateful to all those who read the manuscript,
and made helpful suggestions, especially to
Barbara Adams and our daughters Patti and
Jane. I am particularly grateful to Mr. Allan
Sloane for his friendship, enthusiasm, his
perceptive comments and for just BE-ing who
he is. In addition, I am grateful to my son Jim,
who helped in the final preparation for lettering,
and I am very appreciative of the sensitive,
careful editing of Dr. Harry Shefter and the
encouragement and help of Mr. Doyle
Brentano.

I would like to express my thanks to Dr.
George O'Neill, Ph.D. who has provided practical
help and demonstrated the spirit of integrity of
which he writes. I am grateful to Mr. Lawrence
Hill for his initial faith in publishing the
manuscript. Special thanks are also felt for
Ray Freiman whose work in producing this
book has provided the ideal in a creative
relationship—without diminishing either person
he has made it possible for both of us to
express our selves.

8

FOREWORD

Human Be-ing is a statement about the self and others that can be clearly and readily understood by every reader, young or old. The author uses drawings to emphasize the "meanings" he is putting forth in the various problem areas of *being a human*. We are not born human — we are born homo sapiens with the *capacity* to be taught to be a human, to be taught human-ness. Thus each and every one of us is the product of our culture — its themes, its values, its myths and misbeliefs, its ideals, ritual, tradition, history and more important, its *change*. Thus we are products of our culture while society is the transmitter of this cultural content, shaping and molding each of us from birth — our personality, our character structure, our mental and emotional sets. If we can become whole persons — an integrated self — we can reach a level of maturity and growth that will continue to evolve throughout life.

It is not easy to overcome the shoulds and shouldn'ts of our cultural imperatives that strongly influence our behavior patterns and shape our perception of the reality in which we live. But it is essential if we are to establish a harmony of interaction between the self and the environment — and this includes other people, places, ideas and things. This interaction is so fraught with the myths, outdated norms and accelerated techno-cultural change occurring in our society today that our perceptions are often distorted and our interpretations (particularly in human interaction and communication) invalid. Consequently human relationships break down on many levels — problems are escalated to crises, and crises multiply one on top of the other until we are lost in a vortex of frustration and confusion. We try to find an answer, we seek for a direction — but we are caught in an involuted syndrome of the disparity between the value system we have learned and the behavior corresponding to it, and a changed world in which some values seem no longer to apply.

If we are to build a bridge between the old and the new cultural and societal reality in which we exist, we must begin with human relationships. That is what this book is about; how to grow as a person through better communication — how to break through the power struggle between two people, whether they are mates, family, friends or co-workers — how to accept our own emotions, good or bad, instead of letting society define how we should feel about ourselves — how to continue growth and growing even though it may be painful at times — how to communicate effectively, listening openly to what others have to say and caring for the feelings that underlie their statements — how to seek information in an exchange rather than letting emotionality and presumption cloud the message or break down communication. All of these concepts are useful in helping each of us to know and accept ourselves so that we can better know and understand others.

We have to respect our own self before we can begin to respect the self of others. The recognition of a universal and basic dignity of mankind in each human being is confirmation of our own inherent dignity.

This book may look simple since the drawings clearly reinforce the meaning and concepts the author is presenting. But it is a book to be worked with, and its value lies in the clarity of expression of those humanistic concepts that can lead to *human* BE-ing in its fullest range of growth, understanding and fulfillment.

GEORGE C. O'NEILL
Professor of Anthropology.
The City College, New York
January 1974

INTRODUCTION

○ CONTRAST

○ ON - VOLUME

○ BRIGHTNESS

○ HORIZONTAL HOLD   ○ VERTICAL HOLD

The control knobs of a television set make it possible to enjoy the use of a very complicated instrument that we do not fully understand.

While occasionally problems arise in a TV set which need the work of a specialist, sometimes by consulting an instruction manual conditions can be greatly improved.

In our relationships as human beings, problems also arise which require the help of a specialist. At other times, understanding some principles about ourselves can bring about improvements.

This is an "instruction manual" on human be-ing; not a textbook on major internal repairs. Its purpose is to help provide a clearer picture of how relationships grow and improve.

This book is about
the relationship

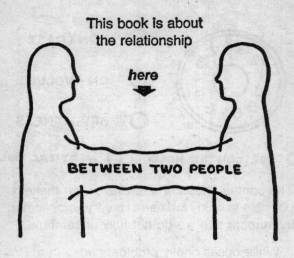

here

BETWEEN TWO PEOPLE

and especially about problems
created when
one person
has some
sort
of
POWER
and
the other one
doesn't.

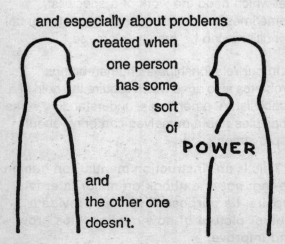

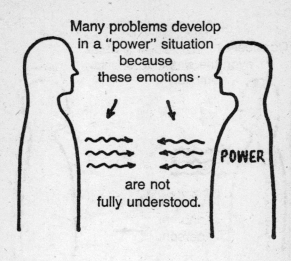

Many problems develop
in a "power" situation
because
these emotions ·

are not
fully understood.

POWER

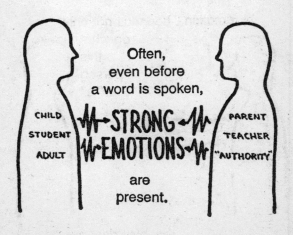

Often,
even before
a word is spoken,

CHILD
STUDENT
ADULT

STRONG
EMOTIONS

PARENT
TEACHER
"AUTHORITY"

are
present.

17

Consider even the simplest emotion

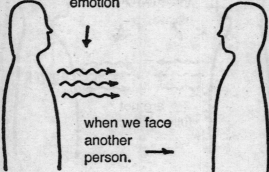

when we face another person. →

This emotion depends not only on what this person "is"

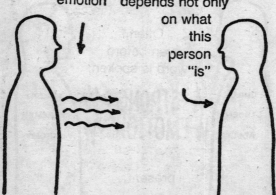

but also depends on ...

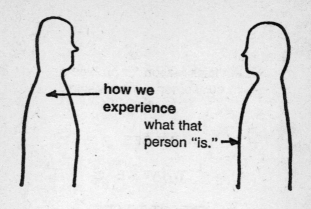

how we
experience
what that
person "is."

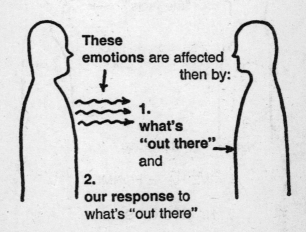

These
emotions are affected
then by:

1.
what's
"out there"
and

2.
our response to
what's "out there"

19

A major reason for problems
in our personal relationships
is that

WE SEE

WHAT WE

EXPECT TO SEE

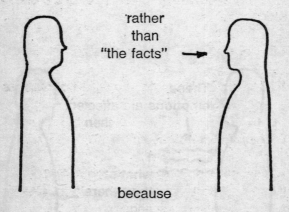

rather
than
"the facts" →

because

WE HAVE FORMED

HABITS OF SEEING

For example:

Do you see anything unusual about the above statement?

Look again.

If it still looks all right to you read it once more . . . carefully.

Did you notice the second "A"?

Almost everybody gets it wrong at first. Why? — Because we have a habit of seeing what we expect to see.

We give the phrase a "meaning" based on our past experience and leave out anything that doesn't fit in with that meaning.

So also . . .

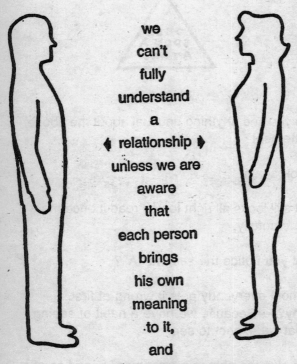

we
can't
fully
understand
a
◀ relationship ▶
unless we are
aware
that
each person
brings
his own
meaning
to it,
and
leaves out things that
don't fit in with that meaning.

CHAPTER I

TRANSFERENCE AND POWER STRUGGLES

We all tend to look for a *"familiar type"* in persons we meet — and to leave out those qualities we don't expect in "that type."

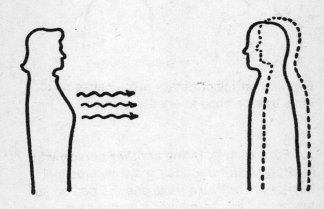

WITHOUT BEING AWARE OF IT
we may *transfer* to another person
emotions and *responses*
we once had towards someone else.

This process is appropriately called
"TRANSFERENCE"

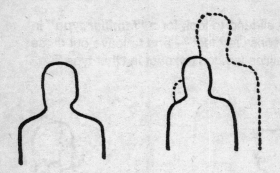

Even rather minor details might cause us to have transference to another person.

. . . For example, facing **another person who is sitting behind a desk** may make us feel inferior . . . or cause us to see the person as having abilities he may or may not have.

. . . Or if **the other person reminds us of someone we admire,** we may be less critical of that person than of someone else.

. . . Or we may see **a large quiet person** as being critical of us when that may not be true at all.

26

"Transference" occurs because the human mind works much like a computer, in which "automatic reactions" are stored away for use as needed . . .

We make our actions "automatic" so that we no longer have to repeat "thinking through the details"

for example . . .

In *learning to drive a car*
we must first think
of each part individually

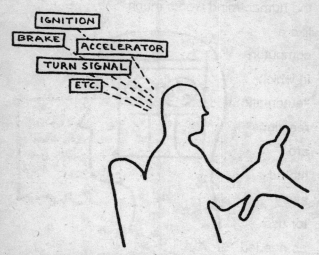

. . . but *once these things are*
"programmed" into our minds
we are free to concentrate on
other things:
conversation,
the radio,
scenery,
etc.
we learn to relate to the car
automatically, "UNCONSCIOUSLY"

28

In a similar way we relate to other activities in AUTOMATIC or "UNCONSCIOUS" ways:

In writing

we don't have to keep thinking about how to form each letter and word; we concentrate on the ideas and the writing comes to us "automatically."

IN READING, words trigger certain automatic thoughts in our memories because we have trained our minds to respond in a certain way.

IN EATING,

our attention tends to focus on the taste, rather than on how to lift food to our mouth, and how to chew and swallow it.

We have programmed ourselves in thousands of ways . . . created habits to make life easier . . . so that we no longer have to think about **HOW** to do these things.

In summary then, our "unconscious mind" serves a useful purpose, (freeing the conscious mind for other tasks), but it also creates problems in our relationships through

TRANSFERENCE
IN
WHICH
WE
"TRANSFER"
AN

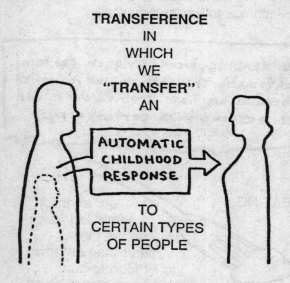

AUTOMATIC CHILDHOOD RESPONSE

TO
CERTAIN TYPES
OF PEOPLE

**WITHOUT BEING
AWARE OF IT.**

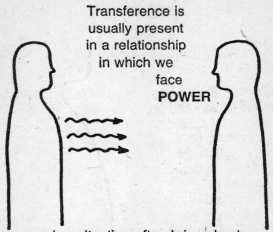

Transference is
usually present
in a relationship
in which we
face
POWER

such a situation often brings back
CHILDHOOD EMOTIONS
such as

"a sense of
futility"
and
"a longing
to be the
one in power"

31

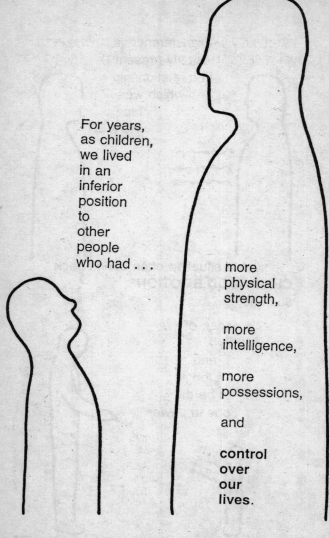

For years,
as children,
we lived
in an
inferior
position
to
other
people
who had . . .

more
physical
strength,

more
intelligence,

more
possessions,

and

**control
over
our
lives**.

Gradually we figured out the best ways to deal with those big people who had the power.

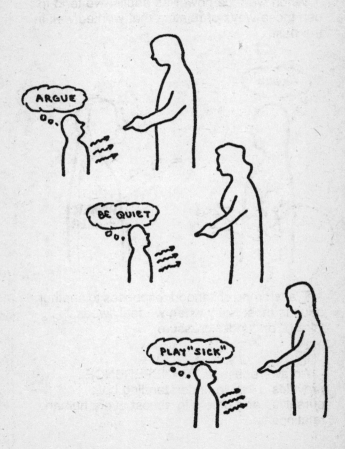

When we face power as adults, we tend to use those ways of relating that worked well in the past.

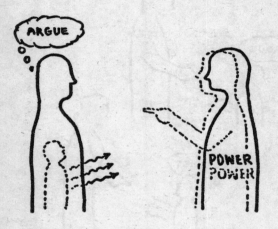

Transferring childhood responses to another adult is most likely when we feel "weak," "tired," or "under pressure."

An awareness of TRANSFERENCE provides a key to understanding both ourselves and others in almost every human relationship.

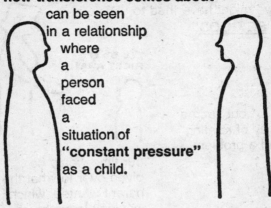

simplified, but specific example of
how transference comes about
can be seen
in a relationship
where
a
person
faced
a
situation of
"constant pressure"
as a child.

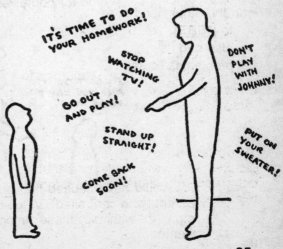

If we had an <u>overdemanding parent</u>, we probably tried to handle it in various ways as a child:

For example . . .
we might have tried to
<u>"BE GOOD"</u>

I'LL DO IT
RIGHT AWAY!

. . . but such a
"way of relating"
had a problem . . .

our time would be
given over to what the
parent wanted, which
wouldn't leave much
time for ourselves.

on the other hand . . .
to **<u>REBEL</u>**
also had its
problems. To say . . .

I WON'T DO IT!
AND YOU CAN'T
MAKE ME!

. . . would have caused that powerful
parent (who controlled TV, ice cream,
etc.) to withhold those things we
wanted.

The most effective method of relating to an over demanding parent was often <u>**DELAY**</u>.

"I'll do it " — gained parent's approval
"...LATER" — gained time for ourselves.

Once "the best way of relating" was discovered, we tended to program the *automatic response* that most easily fit that type of relationship:

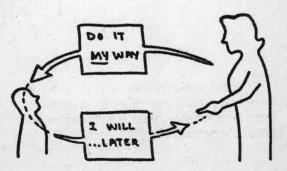

Throughout life we tend to repeat the most effective ways of relating when we face similar situations:

Of course, sometimes delays are very necessary. However, if every demand produces a delay, then transference is probably present.

ANOTHER EXAMPLE OF
how transference comes about
can be seen in a relationship

in
which
a
person
had a
background
where people
QUICKLY
RESPONDED
TO HIS
NEEDS.

When we have had such a childhood we
tend to be impatient as adults, but also
"spontaneous" and "charming" because we
didn't have a constant struggle to get power.

Childhood struggles would only occur when
the parent "reached the limit" and refused to
"give in."

At that point a "temper
tantrum" or an accusation
"You don't love me"

was probably
very effective
in regaining
power.

39

If we had parents who "gave in" easily, we are likely to interpret even reasonable needs of another as proof that the other "does not care." We may not see ourselves as acting in self-centered and impulsive ways.

> IF YOU REALLY LOVED ME, YOU'D GET THAT NEW CAR!

OR

> WHY ARE YOU MAKING SUCH A BIG DEAL ABOUT MY BEING LATE?

OR

> WHY DO WE HAVE TO DO IT _YOUR_ WAY?

Surprisingly, people who have had parents who were "easy" on them are often attracted to people whose parents were overdemanding. They see characteristics in that type of person that they themselves would like to have . . . stability . . . order . . . dependability . . . (which often *are* present). The person with the overdemanding parent likes a person with "spontaneity," and the "security" of the familiar demanding atmosphere he knew as a child.

Power struggles come about most vividly when each person has transference to the other, and uses "seemingly logical" but childish maneuvers in a power situation:

**WHAT
THEN
CAN
WE
DO
ABOUT
IT?**

INSTEAD
OF
A

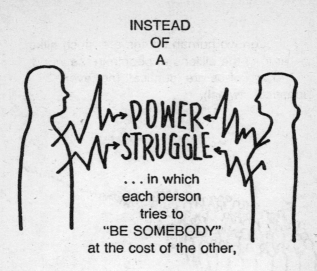

POWER-
STRUGGLE

. . . in which
each person
tries to
"BE SOMEBODY"
at the cost of the other,

IT IS POSSIBLE TO
**ACT
CREATIVELY**
so that
each person's
BE-ING
enriches
the

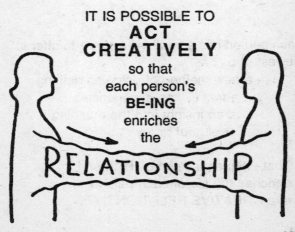

RELATIONSHIP

Although we human beings are much alike
. . . among the billions of people in the world
. . . no two of us are identical, (not even
"identical" twins!)

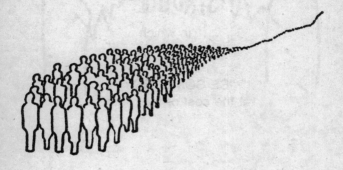

Each person has something *unique* to offer to
the rest of us . . .
        . . . a new method of doing something
        . . . a fact . . . an experience . . .
            . . . an insight into the meaning
                of grief or joy . . .

That uniqueness comes forth and
enriches the life of each person
in a CREATIVE RELATIONSHIP.

TO CREATE
means
"to bring into be-ing."

A CREATIVE RELATIONSHIP

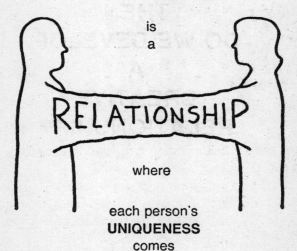

is

a

RELATIONSHIP

where

each person's
UNIQUENESS
comes
into
BE-ING
and enriches the other.

HOW
THEN
DO WE DEVELOP
A
CREATIVE
RELATIONSHIP?

We move *away* from a power struggle and *toward* a creative relationship when we:

1. **TRUST** in the ORGANIC nature of human beings. (p. 50)

2. **PROVIDE** CONDITIONS that make it easy for a person TO BE who he is. (p. 66)

    by   **TRUSTING**   (p. 79)

           LISTENING   (p. 89)

           CLARIFYING   (p. 98)

3. HAVE THE **COURAGE** TO BE. (p. 136)

4. **EXPLORE** ALTERNATIVES with "self" respect. (p. 168)

5. **RISK** a change in our own position. (p. 185)

CHAPTER II

THE ORGANIC NATURE OF HUMAN BEINGS

We act creatively in a
"power" situation when we

1   **TRUST**

IN THE

ORGANIC

NATURE

OF

HUMAN

BEINGS

At times it is difficult to understand how we could trust in any sort of basic goodness in another human being.

Such feelings are quite understandable in light of some of the things we see in "human nature"

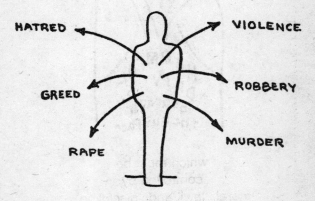

It seems that a person's basic inner nature is filled with destructive desires seeking to escape.

Some religious institutions and
some psychological viewpoints see
basic human nature as
"VOLCANIC"
with

HARMFUL
DRIVES
beneath
the surface

which must be
controlled by
moral "law" and "discipline"
or "channeled" by ego control.
Such an *emphasis* is a

MISUNDERSTANDING

OF THE

BASIC NATURE OF A HUMAN BEING.

Rather than being "VOLCANIC"
(filled with unorganized drives)
HUMAN BEINGS ARE BASICALLY

"ORGANIC"

. . . Systematically moving toward wholeness.

Just as a seed for a plant, or a tree, somehow "knows" what it will someday become, so also, *human beings have within them a sense of "purpose"* — a "knowledge" of what they are *intended to be.*

Just as this

"knowledge"

of

"POTENTIAL

MATURITY"

exists

within

a

SEED,

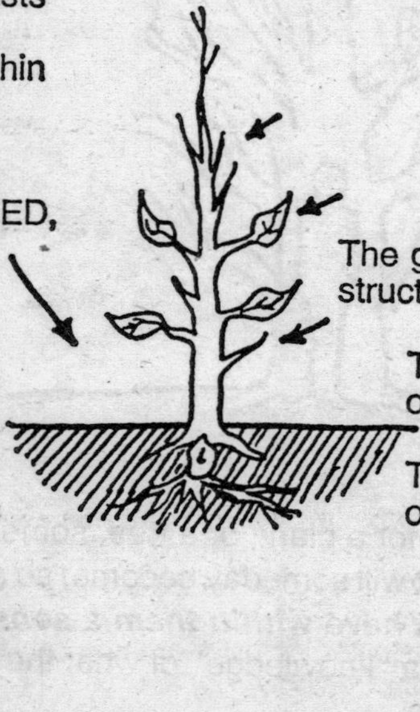

The general
structure

The shape
of the leaves

The texture
of the bark
etc. . . .

so also . . .

... a knowledge* of

POTENTIAL MATURITY

exists

within a

HUMAN BEING

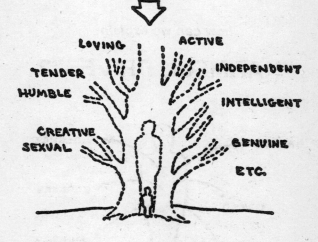

LOVING
ACTIVE
TENDER
INDEPENDENT
HUMBLE
INTELLIGENT
CREATIVE
SEXUAL
GENUINE
ETC.

---

*Known, but not necessarily clearly defined. "The author who benefits you most is not the one who tells you something you did not know before, but the one who gives expression to the truth that has been struggling in you for utterance"

— Oswald Chambers

BUT . . . if a person is

ORGANIC

and potentially "good,"

how can we explain

"HARMFUL DRIVES"?

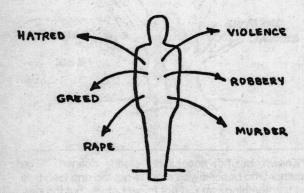

What seem like "harmful drives"
are actually the result of

CUTTING OFF GROWTH

**in much the same way that
a tree is pruned:**

While a
mature tree
might look
something
like this ➧

If too many
branches are
cut off
here

... there may be
so much growth
here

that the tree ends up
"OUT OF BALANCE."

Ideally, we might see our
POTENTIAL MATURITY
as something like this:

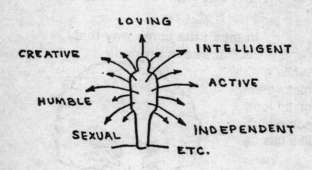

If certain
"branches" of
the personality
are not allowed
to grow,
however . . .

other characteristics
get **out of proportion**
to the rest:

ACTIVE

INDEPENDENT

. . . while being

ACTIVE *and* **INDEPENDENT**

are *good qualities in themselves* . . .

. . . such characteristics **not balanced** by a similar maturity *here*

(in love, tenderness, humility, sexuality etc.)

. . . means problems may be created *here*

ACTIVE

INDEPENDENT

VIOLENCE   GREED   RAPE

Or if

TENDERNESS
and
HUMILITY

get
"OUT OF PROPORTION"   and are *not balanced by active independent qualities*

Other kinds of problems may occur:

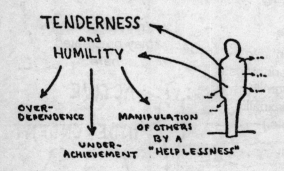

TENDERNESS
and
HUMILITY

OVER-
DEPENDENCE

UNDER-
ACHIEVEMENT

MANIPULATION
OF OTHERS
BY A
"HELPLESSNESS"

In daily life, the person with

ACTIVE
and
INDEPENDENT
qualities
(not balanced by other,
more passive ones),
might express himself
in such attitudes as:

> IF YOU DON'T TAKE CARE OF
> YOURSELF, NO ONE ELSE WILL!

> NOBODY PUSHES _ME_ AROUND!

> I'M NOT A CRY BABY LIKE OTHER PEOPLE!

While an overemphasis
on **TENDERNESS**
and
HUMILITY

might result
in

> WILL YOU HELP ME? I CAN NEVER DO
> ANYTHING RIGHT!

> WHATEVER _YOU_ SAY IS ALL RIGHT.   or

> [blank]   (the silent one)

We get "out of proportion" as human beings because we have been taught that it is *"wrong"* to have certain emotions:

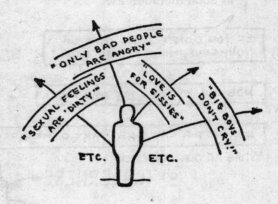

... and so eventually we learn to
hold back growth
in certain branches of our personality
because growth in
these areas seems
either *futile* or
too painful.

When we were children we often blamed ourselves for *having* certain emotions:

While the mature person does **not act on every emotion**, he does try to **accept every emotion** as a part of his **be-ing**.

Once we have learned

to trust in the *basic* goodness

of human nature,

recognizing that

EVERY EMOTION

IS ALL RIGHT

TO HAVE

both

in *ourselves*

and
in *others*

we will
have taken
a huge step
in human relationships.

CHAPTER III

PROVIDING CONDITIONS FOR BE-ING

We also act creatively in
a "power" situation
when we

2

provide

conditions

that make it easy

for a person

to

BE
WHO HE IS

Even though every emotion that we have is good in itself, we are still faced with a very PRACTICAL QUESTION:

In a personal relationship

HOW
DO WE
DEAL WITH
THOSE EMOTIONS
THAT ARE
OUT OF PROPORTION
?

Unfortunately, in dealing with human emotions, we often put the emphasis on "getting things back in shape" by using FORCE (discipline, "law and order," etc.) on those areas of

"trouble"

... rather than by providing conditions for growth here to bring about a **balance** in emotions.

FORCE, (while sometimes helpful), usually deals ONLY WITH SYMPTOMS ... NOT THE SOURCE OF THE PROBLEM.

Generally speaking, problems come about *not because* we were not allowed to *do* something but because we were not allowed to BE somebody.

If the **source** of human problems is found in the fact that we were kept from BEING (certain emotions were not acceptable)

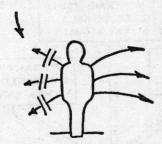

... the **solution** is found in providing conditions so that emotional growth, which once seemed futile or too painful, can begin again ...

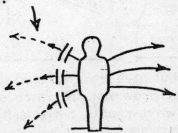

... so the person can move toward being "whole."

Unfortunately, WELL-MEANING adults, who were worried about *"harmful drives,"* attempted to "MOLD US INTO SHAPE" because they feared **human BE-ING.** Such pressure, instead of solving human problems, actually **CREATED THEM!**

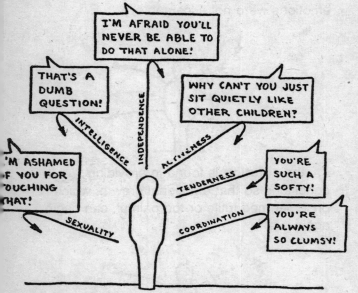

While all of us have probably heard some version of the above words, it is not occasional comments which affect us, but rather it is those phrases which are repeated over and over again which eventually prevent emotional growth in certain areas.

The effect of pressure on emotions might be made clearer if we think of emotions as being like **air** in a child's balloon.

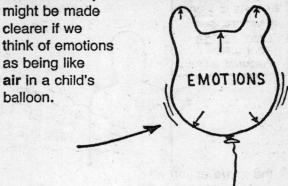

EMOTIONS

Certain areas get "out of proportion"

when **other areas** are **"held in."**

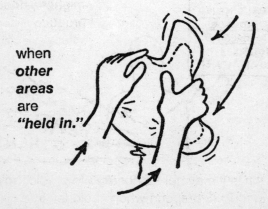

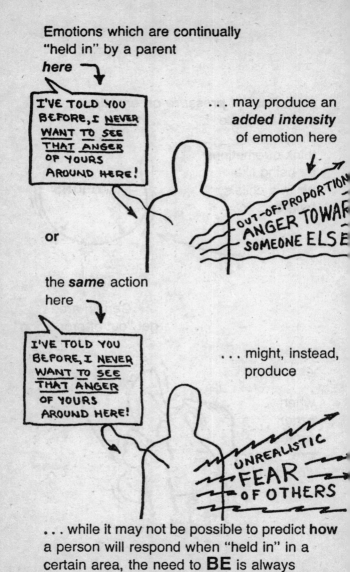

... just as water from a hose
when held back

finds another way of escape, persons who are kept from **BE-ING** in certain ways will find *another way* to BE.

If, as a child
being tender
produced *ridicule* ...

as adults we will
then seek *another*
way of **BE-ING**
that brings *rewards*
without tenderness.

YOU'RE ALWAYS SO SOFT!

HE NEVER MIXES SENTIMENT WITH BUSINESS!

... what is needed in a balloon
to "get things back in shape"
is **not** *more pressure* on
the areas "out of proportion"

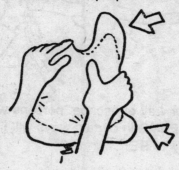

but a RELEASE OF PRESSURE
on the areas "held in"

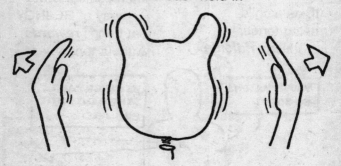

so that it can
be what it is.

So also with human beings . . . what is
needed to "get things back in shape" is **not
more pressure** on the areas that are
out of proportion

but a **release of pressure**
on the areas "held in"

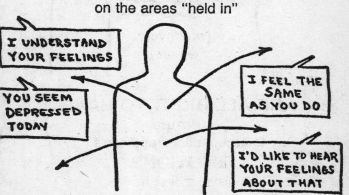

so the person can
BE WHO HE IS

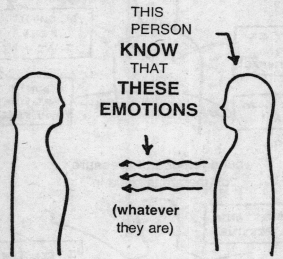

WE "RELEASE PRESSURE" IN
A HUMAN RELATIONSHIP
when we LET

THIS
PERSON
KNOW
THAT
**THESE
EMOTIONS**

(whatever
they are)

ARE ALL RIGHT TO HAVE
because
to accept another person's
EMOTIONS
is to accept his
BE-ING.

CHAPTER IV

TRUSTING, LISTENING, AND CLARIFYING

**THE
CONDITIONS**
which make it easy
for a person
to
BE
who he is

ARE:

TRUSTING,

LISTENING,

and

CLARIFYING

specifically . . .

TRUSTING depends more on what we **are** (our personal viewpoint) than on something we "DO."

Trust is more likely when we understand that another person
1. May be using *unconscious patterns* in relating.
2. Is not basically against us, but *simply trying to* BE.

But

TRUSTING ALSO MEANS

A CONSCIOUS

EFFORT TO

WITHHOLD

JUDGMENT.

WHY a person *has a certain emotion* at a particular time is the result of *many past experiences*

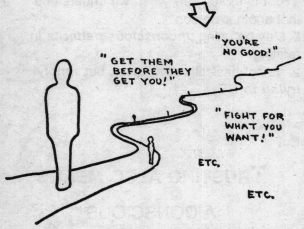

... so that no one has a right to arrogantly inform another **"you *shouldn't* feel *that* way!"**

An emotion is *not what another person is deliberately "doing" to us, but simply what he "HAS" at a particular moment.*

We sometimes quickly PRE-JUDGE a person by **actions alone** without the slightest thought of what might be behind the action.

While our judgment of the person's motive *might* be accurate, to evaluate all the conscious and unconscious motives behind an act (even in our own lives!) is extremely complicated.

Many broken relationships have come about (some of them lasting for years) because, instead of withholding judgment, a person has judged another by actions alone.

While it may be necessary to evaluate a certain **action**.

IT'S WRONG TO STEAL

... and prevent it from happening,

... *it is quite another matter to evaluate another's WORTH AS A HUMAN BEING*

I'M A FAR BETTER PERSON THAN HE IS, BECAUSE I WOULD NEVER DO THAT!

... perhaps with a similar personal history our own actions might even be worse than those of the other person.

It is important to separate the TWO ways of
judging another person:

his
ACTION

and his
BE-ING

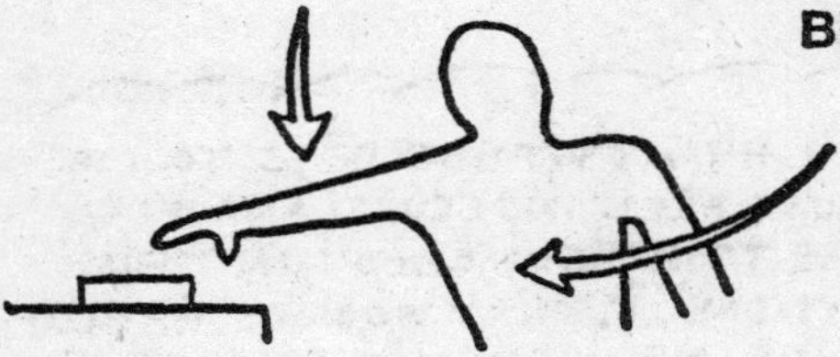

Evaluating an action:

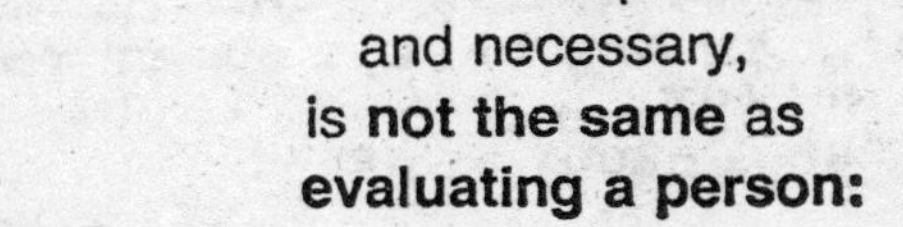

> THAT'S NOT RIGHT, AND I WON'T
> ALLOW HIM TO DO THAT TO ME!

... while important
and necessary,
is **not the same** as
evaluating a person:

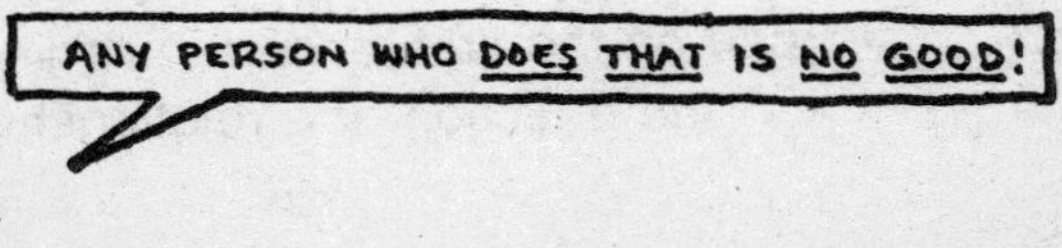

> ANY PERSON WHO <u>DOES THAT</u> IS <u>NO GOOD</u>!

Examples of withholding judgment in typical situations:

> I'M NOT CLEAR WHY HE'S ANGRY. I WONDER IF HE HAS SOME SORT OF TRANSFERENCE TO ME... I'D BETTER TAKE A LOOK AT MYSELF TOO...... I MAY HAVE TRANSFERENCE TO HIM!

> HIS PUSHY ATTITUDE GETS TO ME! HE MUST FEEL INSECURE AND FEEL HE HAS TO BE SOMEBODY IN THIS SITUATION...... THAT SOUNDS RATHER SMUG OF ME ... HUH!... AND I WAS DOING THE SAME THING HE DID—JUST YESTERDAY —... THAT'S INTERESTING!

> WHAT HE'S DOING SEEMS DOWNRIGHT CRUEL TO ME! — I WONDER IF SOMEONE TREATED HIM LIKE THAT WHEN HE WAS A KID!....IN ANY CASE, I OUGHT TO HEAR HIM OUT...... I MIGHT LEARN SOMETHING ABOUT MYSELF!

Such withholding of judgment can be the first step in changing the direction of a relationship.

In thinking about how relationships change, consider the physical law of **inertia**, which tells us that *things tend to continue as they are:*

A wheel spinning in this direction

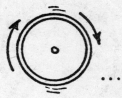

. . . tends to keep going that way.

And a wheel spinning in the opposite direction

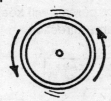

. . . tends to continue *that* way.

Once moving, *a slight push* in the same direction, from either person, *keeps it moving* . . .

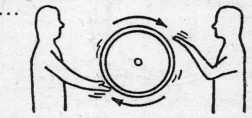

If each continues to push in this way, stopping soon becomes very difficult.

In the world of relationships there seems to be a law of *"emotional inertia"* in which things tend to continue as they are . . .

Once moving in a particular direction a "slight push" from either person will keep things moving in the same direction.

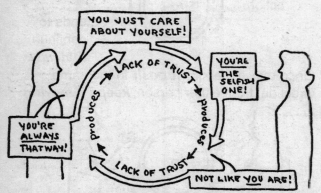

If each continues to "push" in this way, stopping soon becomes extremely difficult, and the chance of reversing the cycle is very unlikely.

BY WITHHOLDING JUDGMENT,

*. . . making the conscious decision
not to act on limited evidence,*
we are, in a sense,
"NOT PUSHING."

While this may not reverse the
cycle, it may **at least permit it
to slow down** so that reversing
may later become possible.

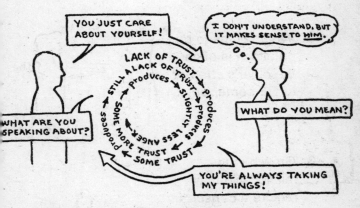

*. . . Once a withholding of judgment is
sensed by the other person, a new
atmosphere is present which prepares the
way for an increasingly creative
relationship.*

TRUSTING, then,

means being **aware** that

1. *Unconscious patterns* are present in the relationship in *both* persons.

2. What seems to be an attack is often the other's *attempt to BE somebody.*

3. Growth in the relationship may require a *conscious effort to withhold judgment* as to "why" the person feels as he does.

In addition to **TRUSTING**, *another condition that makes it easy for a person to BE who he is,*

IS . . .

LISTENING

Real Listening means "tuning in" to what the other person is *feeling* . . .

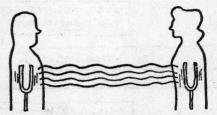

. . . so that we *listen to emotions,* not simply hear "ideas."

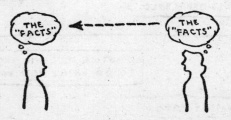

LISTENING means trying to "hear"[i]
the "deeper message" of the emotions:

such as

> IT'S ELEVEN O'CLOCK AND HE'S NOT HERE YET.

SHE SEEMS WORRIED THAT HE'S LATE.

> I'VE REALLY <u>HAD IT</u> WITH JOHN!

SHE'S ANGRY AND FRUSTRATED WITH JOHN.

> SUZIE ALWAYS GETS WHAT <u>SHE</u> WANTS!

HE FEELS HE'S NOT TREATED FAIRLY.

> WELL, <u>ANOTHER</u> WASTED DAY, AS USUAL.

HE SOUNDS DEPRESSED.

> I NOTICE YOU HAD TIME TO DO WHAT <u>YOU</u> WANT!

SHE'S ANGRY WITH ME.

Most of us have been trained to listen to "facts" rather than "feelings."

Actually, human beings are in "stereo"...

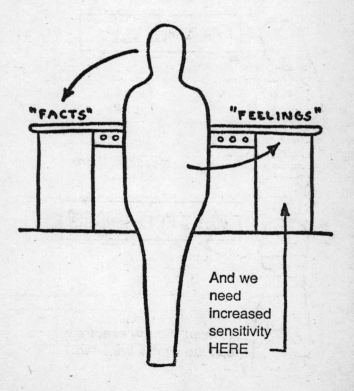

"FACTS"

"FEELINGS"

And we
need
increased
sensitivity
HERE

Sometimes the message communicated by the emotions (through tone and physical expression), is the **complete reverse** of what is said through the **words**:

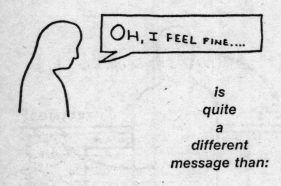

*is
quite
a
different
message than:*

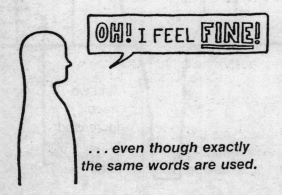

*. . . even though exactly
the same words are used.*

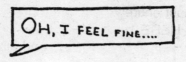

. . . may be a way of
sending **two messages**
at the same time . . .

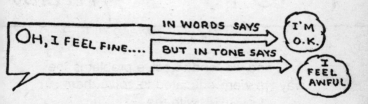

The double message "checks out" (perhaps unconsciously) the other person's depth of listening . . . to see if he cares enough to *really* hear what is being said.

The person who **LISTENS** to the emotional message demonstrates that he *cares* about our BE-ING, and so helps us to be more "whole."

MOST OF US FIND IT DIFFICULT TO
listen to emotions.

Unfortunately, our formal education
has been
almost entirely
HERE

. . . and almost none
of it HERE

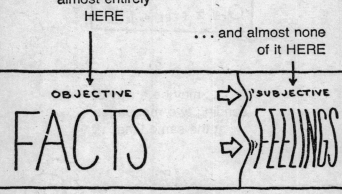

OBJECTIVE

'SUBJECTIVE

FACTS

FEELINGS

. . . and we tend to solve problems the
way we were educated to solve them . . .
with the
⇒ INTELLECT ⇐
without
much reference to

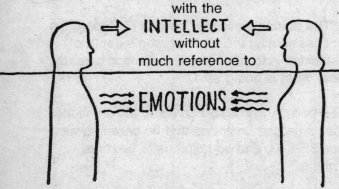

≋ EMOTIONS ≋

Actually, facts and feelings are not so easily separated. *If strong emotions are ignored, communicating* **"THE FACTS"** *becomes* **increasingly difficult:**

Sometimes very intense POWER STRUGGLES occur over issues that seem to be rather trivial.

On a deeper level, it is *not the action* which is taken that is really important, but *what the action means emotionally to each person:*

Arguments over trivials may really be
saying . . .

the message of many arguments
(. . . if only we could hear it!)
is
"I WANT TO BE IMPORTANT TO YOU"

POWER STRUGGLES often end with remarks
such as

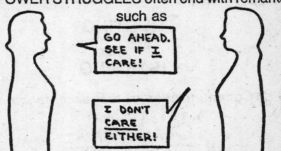

. . . which, interestingly, speaks
not about the "facts,"
but about the **relationship.**

A CREATIVE RELATIONSHIP in which growth is possible occurs when there is . . .

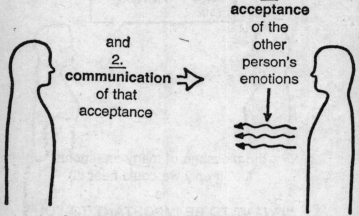

**1.
acceptance**
of the
other
person's
emotions

and
**2.
communication**
of that
acceptance

1. **Acceptance** *of the other person's emotions*
comes about through

TRUSTING
and
LISTENING

2. Communication *of that acceptance*
comes about through
CLARIFYING

— making clear
to the other person
what has been heard.

To **CLARIFY** is helpful to

the listener

because

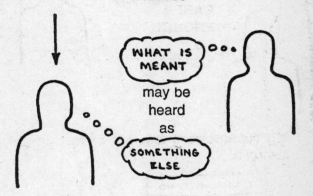

and *making clear what "facts" have been heard can prevent misunderstandings.*

BUT..

the greatest value

of CLARIFYING

IS ...

... that it lets **the speaker**

Know that
the other
person

**CARES
ENOUGH
TO
LISTEN.**

It is not enough to say:

I UNDERSTAND.

We must *demonstrate that we understand* by *making clear* WHAT *has been heard:*

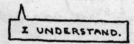

IT SOUNDS AS IF YOU ARE VERY HURT
ABOUT WHAT I HAVE DONE.

To continually feed back each phrase
would be irritating if there is already good
communication. It is usually unnecessary to
clarify until the speaker has strong
emotions that need to be heard.

100

We demonstrate that we care enough to listen when we "tune in," not simply to the "factual" message, . . .

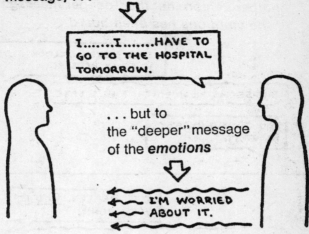

. . . but to
the "deeper" message
of the *emotions*

When a person has strong emotions, making clear that we have heard the "factual" message . . .

> I HEAR YOU SAYING THAT YOU'RE GOING TO THE HOSPITAL.

is not of much value . . .

. . . but making clear that the **PERSON** has been heard . . .

> YOU SOUND CONCERNED ABOUT IT.

is *tremendously helpful.*

CLARIFYING then, means *making clear to another person that the "deeper message" of the emotions has been heard*

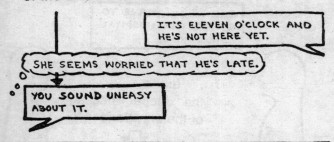

IT'S ELEVEN O'CLOCK AND HE'S NOT HERE YET.

SHE SEEMS WORRIED THAT HE'S LATE.

YOU SOUND UNEASY ABOUT IT.

I'VE REALLY HAD IT WITH JOHN!

SHE'S ANGRY AND FRUSTRATED WITH HIM.

IT SOUNDS AS IF YOU'VE REACHED YOUR LIMIT WITH JOHN!

SUZIE ALWAYS GETS WHAT SHE WANTS!

HE FEELS HE'S NOT BEING TREATED FAIRLY.

YOU FEEL SHE GETS MORE THAN YOU DO!

WELL, ANOTHER WASTED DAY, AS USUAL

...E SOUNDS DEPRESSED

...OU SOUND DEPRESSED

I NOTICE YOU HAD TIME TO DO WHAT YOU WANTED!

SHE'S ANGRY WITH ME

YOU FEEL I HAVE TIME FOR MYSELF, BUT NOT FOR YOU

Clarifying does *not* mean
"I agree with your opinion"
but rather:

"I HEAR YOU SAYING. . ."

NOTE: Sincerity in trying to listen is vital. If the other person feels manipulated and angry, the listener is probably just "using a technique" (clarifying, without trust and listening). Paraphrasing rather than parroting helps the other person know that real understanding is there — not just an "automatic replay" of words.

103

Unfortunately . . .
when there are strong emotions
in another person, we tend to
feel that the best way to deal
with the situation
is

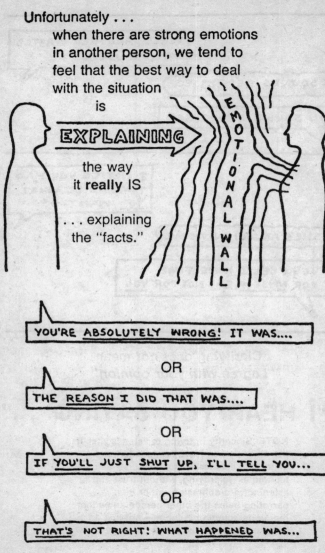

EXPLAINING

the way
it **really** IS

. . . explaining
the "facts."

EMOTIONAL WALL

YOU'RE <u>ABSOLUTELY</u> <u>WRONG!</u> IT WAS....

OR

THE <u>REASON</u> I DID THAT WAS....

OR

IF <u>YOU'LL</u> JUST <u>SHUT</u> <u>UP,</u> I'LL <u>TELL</u> YOU...

OR

<u>THAT'S</u> NOT RIGHT! WHAT <u>HAPPENED</u> WAS...

104

In reality, *it is the reverse of our natural tendency to "explain," which brings about communication.*

It is only *after* we express our *emotional understanding* for the other person . . .

. . . that the other person
is **READY TO** "HEAR" facts

"HEARING" comes about in this order:

> **first** — EMOTIONAL UNDERSTANDING
> Then — "The facts"
>
>   **not**
>
> First — "The facts"
> Then — EMOTIONAL UNDERSTANDING

We might imagine emotions as being

like
steam
in a
pressure
cooker

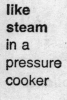
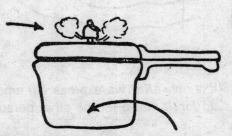

... and **_"the facts" like the food inside._**

To avoid an explosion, we first reduce the emotional "pressure." Once the "pressure" of the emotions has been released it is possible to take a look at "the facts" with a minimum amount of trouble.

I'LL SAY IT WOULD! ALL WE EVER DO IS SEE *YOUR* FRIENDS!

YOU'RE TIRED OF SEEING MY FRIENDS ALL THE TIME!

WELL, IT'S NOT THAT I DON'T LIKE THEM, BUT WE HAVEN'T SEEN GERRY AND PAT FOR MONTHS!

At this point, the "pressure" has come down to the level where the listener could express some of his own specific needs. Even so, it is important to continue confirming that the "deeper message" of the emotions is being heard.

YOU MISS THE RELATIONSHIP YOU HAD WITH THEM!

YES, I DO MISS THEM. I LIKE THEM BOTH A LOT!

WELL, TO SEE THEM RIGHT AWAY, WE'D HAVE TO CHANGE OUR PLANS FOR THIS WEEK!

I WOULDN'T WANT TO DO THAT, BUT I WOULD LIKE TO SEE THEM AGAIN SOON.

O.K., I DIDN'T KNOW IT MEANT THAT MUCH TO YOU!

YEAH, IT REALLY DOES. I'M GLAD YOU UNDERSTAND HOW I FEEL!

While in this case the reduction of "pressure" was fairly rapid, the time it takes to move from "emotion" to "logic" varies. If the original emotion is very strong, it will take longer.

In clarifying, then, it is important to simply *describe,* in our own words, *as accurately as possible, what the other person is feeling.*

Generally speaking,
    questions . . .
        comments . . .
            and *"explaining"*

    cause complications,

        and a delay in reducing
        emotional pressure.

> YOU ALWAYS DID THINK I WAS STUPID.

> DIDN'T I TELL YOU HOW SMART YOU WERE, JUST LAST WEEK?

This kind of question tends to be of little use. It simply leads to an argument over "facts," where neither person listens, and "yes, but . . . " is used frequently.

> YOU FEEL THAT I SEE YOU AS STUPID.

is a description of what the other person feels, and promotes communication.

> EVERY TIME I DO SOMETHING NICE FOR YOU, YOU COME BACK WITH SOME NASTY REMARK!

> MAYBE I WOULDN'T IF YOU DIDN'T NAG SO MUCH!

This "explanation" and attack is far less helpful than:

> YOU FEEL I'M UNAPPRECIATIVE AND CRITICAL.

> I SEE WE'RE DOING IT YOUR WAY AGAIN!

> WHAT DO YOU MEAN? WE NEVER DO IT MY WAY!

. . . this again leads to a discussion of "facts" and an escalation of emotions.
BUT

> YOU FEEL I'M NOT VERY THOUGHTFUL OF YOU?

. . . promotes communication.

111

> YOU'RE _ALWAYS_ TRYING TO TELL ME HOW TO RUN MY LIFE!

> THAT'S _NOT_ _TRUE!_

Comments like this generally create further emotional problems. While clarifying "facts" may be useful at a later time, the above response almost always causes frustration in the other person.

> YOU FEEL I'M BOSSY.

is better.

IN A
RELATIONSHIP
IT IS
NOT

that are of
primary importance
BUT
HOW EACH PERSON

≋FEELS≋

ABOUT THE FACTS

Effective listening
means
demonstrating that we
care enough to hear
the other's viewpoint.

LOVE
IS
PAYING
ATTENTION.

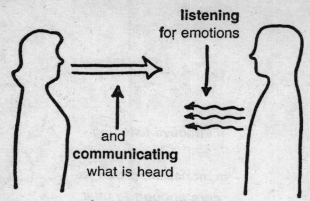

listening
for emotions

**and
communicating**
what is heard

does not "just happen."
IT REQUIRES

AN ACT OF THE <u>WILL</u>

in which
this person,

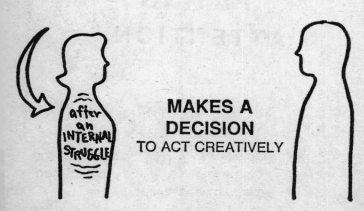

after
an
INTERNAL
STRUGGLE

**MAKES A
DECISION**
TO ACT CREATIVELY

An act of the will
is needed to
listen
for emotions
and to
communicate
understanding

especially
when

ANGRY
EMOTIONS

are directed
toward us

. . . those **angry emotions**

trigger
very strong emotions
in ourselves.

We are "reminded" of the childhood situations
when the "big people" were angry with us, *and
our* **be-ing** *was threatened.*

The inner struggle to act creatively might be like this:

ALL RIGHT! IF **YOU** SAY SO:

UH-OH! I CAN FEEL MY ANGER COMING UP.......I'D SURE LIKE TO BLAST HIM BACK........I WONDER HOW MUCH OF THIS ANGER IN ME IS JUSTIFIED BY THIS SITUATION? ...... I MIGHT BE USING AN AUTOMATIC WAY OF RELATING TO HIM.......OR HE MIGHT BE RESPONDING IN SOME UNCONSCIOUS WAY TO ME......... WHO KNOWS?..........IN ANY CASE, HE BELIEVES HE'S FAIR AND RIGHT. ....I CAN'T SEE HOW HE COULD... ......THE "CHILD" IN ME IS PUSHING ME TO TELL HIM OFF ANYWAY.........MY "ADULT" SIDE SAYS LISTEN TO WHAT HE IS SAYING ....HE SOUNDS ANGRY AS HELL AT ME... ....HE SAYS HE'LL DO IT, BUT HE'S REALLY STEAMING........WELL, ONE OF US HAS TO DO THE LISTENING FIRST......IT MIGHT AS WELL BE ME........*

YOU SOUND VERY ANGRY WITH ME!

116

* (While the actual inner struggle may not be as detailed as this before a word is spoken, the type of struggle is indicated above.)

And other "acts of the will" would be needed to continue acting creatively. It is *most necessary*, but also most *difficult* when we are under attack:

> YES, I'M ANGRY.....YOU GIVE ME ALL THE DIRTY JOBS!

> HOW CAN HE SAY THAT?.....THAT'S NOT THE WAY I SEE IT....I CAN FEEL MY ANGER COMING UP....HE REALLY BELIEVES THAT I'M WRONG.....I WANT TO EXPLAIN BUT HE'S NOT READY TO HEAR ME YET.... HE FIRST HAS TO KNOW THAT I UNDERSTAND HOW HE FEELS.....

> YOU FEEL THAT I'M BEING UNFAIR?...

> THAT'S RIGHT! ALL YOU CARE ABOUT IS WHAT'S IN IT FOR YOU

> AFTER ALL I'VE DONE FOR HIM!.....WELL, IT'S NOT "THE FACTS" AS I SEE THEM THAT MATTERS BUT UNDERSTANDING HIS FEELINGS.....

> I HEAR YOU SAYING THAT I JUST CARE ABOUT MYSELF.

> DAMN RIGHT! I'VE JUST ABOUT HAD IT WITH YOU!

> I'M GETTING ANGRY AGAIN MYSELF..... BUT I'D BETTER LISTEN TO HIM

> YOU SOUND AS IF YOU'RE REALLY DISGUSTED WITH ME.....

ETC.
ETC.

Generally, it is simpler and clearer if **one person** concentrates on **listening** and **clarifying** (for at least five or ten minutes, but possibly even for an hour, or more in some circumstances).

While this may seem "unfair" for the one listening, it's eventually easier for both. Each person's ability to hear **increases when one or the other focuses on paying attention** while the other talks.

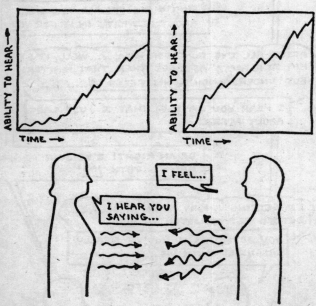

To repeat . . .

Listening for EMOTIONS
and making clear that
we understand
is

MOST DIFFICULT

WHEN WE ARE

UNDER

ATTACK

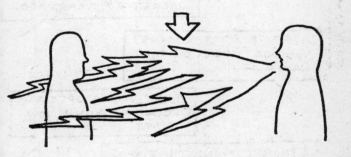

but when this happens, to **listen
with understanding** *without
"correcting facts"* is also
MOST NECESSARY

EXPLAINING "FACTS"· WHEN WE ARE ATTACKED PRODUCES A DIALOGUE SUCH AS THIS

YOU NEVER DID KNOW HOW TO HANDLE MONEY!

WELL, I NEVER SPEND MONEY ON MYSELF LIKE YOU DO!

YEAH? HOW ABOUT THAT NEW OVERCOAT YOU JUST GOT?

THAT WASN'T AN OVERCOAT IT WAS A RAINCOAT — THE FIRST ONE I'VE BOUGHT IN FOUR YEARS.

YOU BOUGHT THAT BLUE JACKET 2½ YEARS AGO.

WHAT ABOUT THE MONEY YOU JUST SPENT ON THAT NEW SUIT?

THAT WAS A SPECIAL OCCASION. YOU KNOW THAT!

I DIDN'T THINK THAT WAS SUCH A SPECIAL OCCASION!

IT CERTAINLY WAS! DON'T YOU REMEMBER...

and it can go on, and on, and on . . .
with increasing frustration.

ON THE OTHER HAND

DESCRIBING THE OTHER'S EMOTIONAL VIEWPOINT

TENDS TO PRODUCE A DIALOGUE
SUCH AS THIS

YOU NEVER DID KNOW HOW TO HANDLE MONEY!

YOU FEEL I'VE SPENT MONEY IN FOOLISH WAYS.

"FOOLISH WAYS" IS RIGHT! HOW ABOUT THAT NEW OVERCOAT YOU JUST GOT?

YOU FEEL THAT WAS A RATHER STUPID WAY TO SPEND MONEY.

I'M FED UP WITH THE WAY YOU'RE ALWAYS WASTING MONEY.

YOU SOUND AS IF YOU'VE "HAD IT" WITH ME!

Because of our natural tendency to "blast" back when criticized, clarifying is liable to be heard as phony. It is not. Quietly listening with **TRUST** means respect for the person, which is the very opposite of manipulation.

121

YES! WE WOULDN'T BE IN THIS MESS IF IT WEREN'T FOR YOU.

YOU FEEL I'M TO BLAME FOR EVERYTHING!

I'M NOT SAYING EVERYTHIN IS ALL YOUR FAULT......
......MAYBE I WAS A LITTLE HASTY IN BUYING THAT NEV SUIT......

YOU FEEL YOU MAY BE PARTLY RESPONSIBLE, TOO.

NOT LIKE YOU ARE..... BUT MAYBE A LITTLE.....
......THE MAIN THING, NO' THOUGH, IS TO FIGURE OUT WHAT TO DO ABOUT THE BI BILL THAT'S DUE NEXT WEE

When what we have said is reflected back to us, we hear what we have said a second time, and begin to reevaluate our words and clarify our thoughts and feelings.

Clarifying does **not** mean "I agree with your opinion." It does mean *non-judgmental understanding of feelings.*

122

While communication becomes a problem when we are attacked, it is also difficult to clarify what we hear *when the other person is feeling* DEPRESSED.

Our tendency is to want to **change** the other person by expressing what seems true to us rather than allowing the person to work out his own problem

Trying to protect a person from sorrow, for example instead of being helpful may actually make him feel *more lonely:*

CHEER UP! THINGS AREN'T REALLY THAT BAD!

HE JUST DOESN'T UNDERSTAND!

If we can only **trust** in *the other person's capacity to solve his own problem,* and listen attentively, and respond sincerely, we find that the other person, by putting his problem into words to a listening ear, is finding *strength in himself* and *moving toward a solution.*

123

The following is the type of TRUSTING, LISTENING, and CLARIFYING which promotes movement toward a solution.

Note that the one listening, instead of "giving answers," simply tries to **"be with"** the other person by putting his feelings into words.

The listener's depth of understanding is evident in the fact that instead of mechanically repeating what is said, the emotion is expressed in the listener's own words.

YES... THREE PEOPLE IN MY UNIT HAVE ALREADY LEFT.

IT SEEMS IT'S GETTING TOO CLOSE FOR COMFORT!

I WONDER IF _I'M_ NEXT.

YOU FEEL YOU MIGHT LOSE YOUR JOB?

YES! AND THERE'S NOT MUCH AVAILABLE IN MY LINE OF WORK.

I HEAR YOU SAYING YOU DON'T HAVE MUCH HOPE IN FINDING SOMETHING ELSE.

It may seem that the above responses are simply promoting "negative thoughts" instead of offering encouragement and practical advice. Yet, *it is vitally important to continue this type of response until the person in need knows that his emotional viewpoint is understood and accepted.*

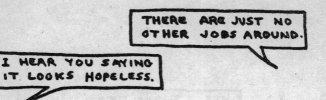

THERE ARE JUST NO
OTHER JOBS AROUND.

I HEAR YOU SAYING
IT LOOKS HOPELESS.

Eventually the other person will begin to "hear himself," and through explaining will clarify what he is saying, and perhaps move toward some tentative positive statements.

I WOULDN'T SAY "HOPELESS"
BUT IT'S PRETTY BAD.

YOU FEEL IT'S NOT
COMPLETELY HOPELESS.

IT'S STILL PLENTY BAD.

Gradually, the person in need will be able to explore possible solutions:

IS THERE ANY WAY YOU
COULD GET TRAINED IN
SOMETHING ELSE?

HOWEVER, we are seldom ready to hear about solutions from others until we know we have been heard by them.

126

It may require a great deal of listening before a person can move from his emotional feelings to the point where various choices can be explored . . .

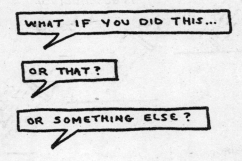

WHAT IF YOU DID THIS...

OR THAT?

OR SOMETHING ELSE?

Even when such phrases are used, we need to resist the temptation to say . . .

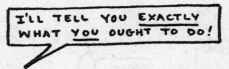

I'LL TELL YOU EXACTLY WHAT YOU OUGHT TO DO!

. . . which tends to make the person feel he is not capable of solving his own problems . . . and produces a lack of confidence in his own ability when other problems arise.

"CLARIFYING" — demonstrating that we understand — helps another person come into BE-ING.

Just as *watering a plant*

is essential for

be-ing

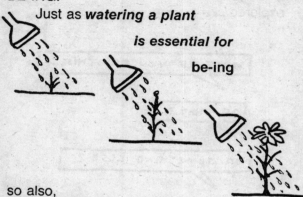

so also,
clarifying that we
understand another person's emotions
helps that person come into BE-ING

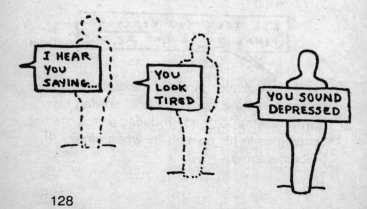

As children we find it necessary to affirm that we are of value, over and over again. When others pay attention to us, it affirms that we **are** somebody:

This does not mean that we must constantly pay attention to children . . . to do so **continually** would be to give up a part of our **own** BE-ING, and make us resentful toward the children. The child soon senses phony love. It's better to tell the child ∴.

I CAN'T WATCH NOW. I'LL SEE IT LATER.

. . . and later give FULL attention. Full attention for a short time is far better than half attention for a longer period.

UH HUH . . . . UH HUH . . . . UH HUH instead of being helpful, may be very destructive in a relationship with children or adults.

129

When a person *knows* that he has been understood, a new atmosphere has been created, and communication not only begins, but **tends to continue** . . .

. . . for just as there is an "emotional inertia" with a *negative* effect . . .

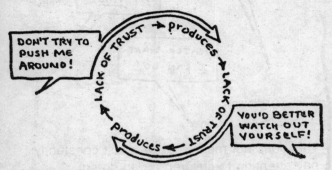

"emotional inertia" can also have a positive effect . . .

TRUST brings back **TRUST** to us.

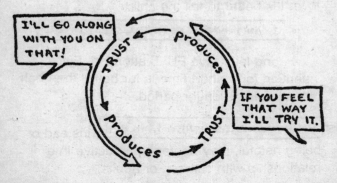

For the sake of the relationship, it may be necessary, temporarily, *not to act on our emotions*, and listen to the other person . . .

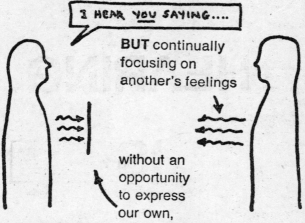

I HEAR YOU SAYING....

BUT continually focusing on another's feelings

without an opportunity to express our own,

will eventually lead to frustration.

Everyone must have a place where his own feelings may be expressed to another person and HEARD.

We gain both insight and strength when someone hears us. It is unfortunate that there are so few listeners . . .

because . . .

HEARING

IS

HEALING

SUMMARY

COMMUNICATION comes about when, through an inner struggle, we seek to **DEMONSTRATE THAT WE CARE** by:

TRUSTING. Making the conscious effort to "withhold judgment" of *why* the other person feels as he does.

LISTENING. Trying to discover what the other person is **feeling**. If uncertain, stating, "I don't understand what you're saying."

CLARIFYING. Clarifying that the "deeper message" has been heard by DESCRIBING ANOTHER'S FEELINGS, as accurately as possible, *without defending ourselves or commenting on what has been said.*
Using such words as: *"You* feel . . . ?, *"You* sound . . .", "I hear *you* saying . . ."
NOTE: To "clarify" does *not* mean "I agree with your opinion. It *does* mean *non-judgmental understanding* of feelings. *Emotions are neither good nor bad, right nor wrong, but simply what we "have" at a particular moment.*

When a person *knows* that we have understood his feelings, a new atmosphere is created, and communication begins.

It is important to be aware that the process of

trusting ... listening ... and clarifying

is not simply a "technique"
but
A MEANS TO A BETTER RELATIONSHIP.
No one likes to feel ...

HE'S USING THAT TECHNIQUE ON ME!

If we feel that way, it's important
to remind ourselves ...

HE'S DOING THAT BECAUSE HE CARES ABOUT OUR RELATIONSHIP.

A useful phrase to communicate **CARING** is

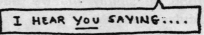

I HEAR <u>YOU</u> SAYING ....

If, in the beginning, the listener keeps responding with these words, he will be clarifying the
relationship for both the speaker *and himself.*

CHAPTER V

HAVING THE COURAGE TO BE

We also *act creatively* in
a "power" situation
when we

3

HAVE

THE

COURAGE

TO BE

OURSELVES

Having the courage

to be

means

having

LOVE

FOR

our

own

''SELF''

Unfortunately many people see

LOVE

as thinking *only* about the person
"out there"

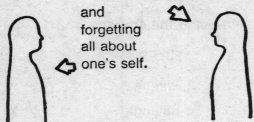

and
forgetting
all about
one's self.

Actually **REAL LOVE** includes

RESPECT for the **"SELF"**
of **ALL** HUMAN BEINGS

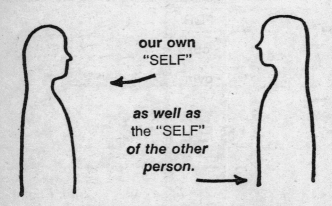

our own
"SELF"

as well as
the "SELF"
*of the other
person.*

"LOVE OTHERS AS YOURSELF."

If we think of love as "giving in to the needs of others" we may actually be more irritating to others than helpful to them. . . .

To simply say

is so much easier for both!

Just as a plant, in seeking to BE, might push its way through some rocks — not allowing the surroundings to keep it from existing — so also, as humans, we have a need to protect ourselves from **"not be-ing."**

"The courage to be is the ethical act in which a man affirms his own being in spite of [the] elements of his existence which conflict with his essential self-affirmation."

— Paul Tillich

Physically, we all occupy a certain area of the earth, which, for that moment, is "our own."

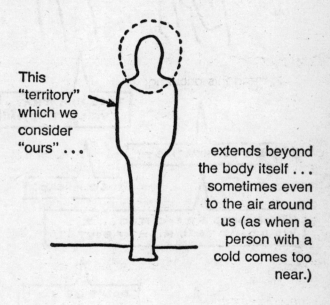

This "territory" which we consider "ours" . . . → extends beyond the body itself . . . sometimes even to the air around us (as when a person with a cold comes too near.)

Our "be-ing" depends on protecting that territory. It is not selfish in a negative sense to simply want to "be." Such "be-ing" is a part of life — in fact it *is* life.

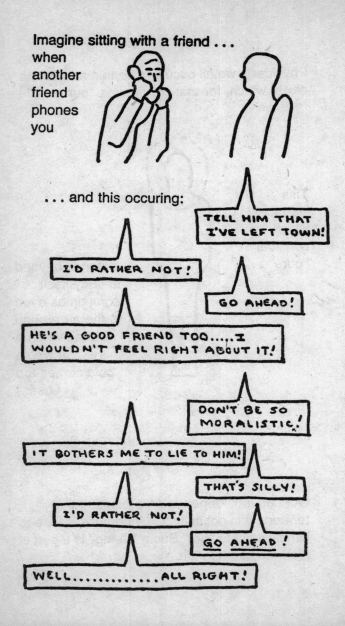

In such a situation, the other
person has invaded your "emotional
territory" and you have given

away a part

of your

"SELF."

Even though you have allowed it to happen,
resentment
will follow . . . toward *yourself*, and *toward the
other person* . . . because there has been a
lack of "SELF" respect on your own part, and
on his as well.

We are actually surrounded by many kinds of territories which affect our be-ing in a variety of ways

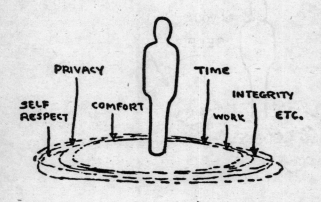

PRIVACY   TIME

SELF
RESPECT   COMFORT   INTEGRITY

WORK   ETC.

If another person *forces himself* into our territory, *even with our permission*, we can expect to feel both anger toward ourselves (for allowing it to happen), and resentment toward the other person (for not respecting our "SELF")

144

MISUNDERSTANDINGS come about because
we **ASSUME** that the other person *should
know* the limits of

OUR TERRITORY

*. . . but what may be an "infringement
of territory" for one person* (as in the
previous example of the phone call),
*may hardly affect
another person in
the same situation:*

TELL HIM I'VE LEFT TOWN!

O.K.!

Because "territories" are not always clearly evident, we have a responsibility to

DEFINE

THAT AREA
WHICH IS OUR

"Territorial limits", both physical, and emotional, are **defined** by the **"ouch!"** line

Our "territory" is that area *within which* another person is causing us *continuous* pain — that area within which our be-ing is affected.

The location of the "ouch!" Line
is determined by the person
WITHIN the territory, rather than
by the person outside of it

... for while
another
person
might
guess
the limits
of another's
territory ...

only the person **within** knows the exact point
where pain is felt.

For example ...

To step on another person's foot
may or may not be painful.
*Only the person whose
territory is being affected
knows the
precise
location
of the
"ouch!" line ...*

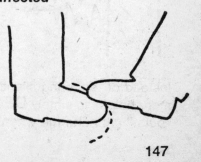

While most of us would have little problem in asking another person to physically "Keep from stepping on our toes," we tend to feel that protecting our *emotional* territory is not "being loving' — that it is "selfish" in the negative sense of the word.

YET ...

To "suffer silently" is not fair either to ourselves *or the other person*, for it creates "underground" problems in the relationship which the other person finds difficult to understand:

Instead of "suffering silently" it is usually far more helpful to simply **DEFINE** that which is "ours." ("It hurts me when you do that.")

DEFINING emotional "ouch!" lines would be seen in statements such as these in which we **make our emotion known:**

> I'M FINDING IT DIFFICULT TO READ WITH THAT MUSIC SO LOUD. WOULD YOU PLEASE TURN IT DOWN A LITTLE.

AND

> I'D RATHER NOT SPEND THE EVENING WITH HIM. WOULD YOU ASK SOMEONE ELSE?

AND

> I'M SORRY, I NEVER LEND THAT TO ANYONE. IT WAS A GIFT FROM A VERY SPECIAL PERSON!

AND

> I CAN'T TALK ANY LONGER WITH YOU NOW. I HAVE SOME THINGS TO DO.

It is ultimately better to let another person know when he is over the "ouch!" line (he may not be aware of it!) than to relate on a basis of false "politeness."

DEFINING OUR TERRITORY, then, simply means *DESCRIBING THAT WHICH IS OUR OWN* ("My feelings are . . .")

WITHOUT
TRYING TO
CHANGE *THE*
OTHER PERSON.

Problems are seldom
solved by words
such as:

IF YOU WOULD JUST....

For most people such a phrase triggers off childhood emotions of inferiority . . .

... and the need to be in power:

and the need to "put down" to regain power:

... and the process is again reversed. Such struggles generally continue with little or no progress, benefiting neither person, and leaving both exhausted and emotionally drained.

On the other hand, if **instead of** giving
"ADVICE"

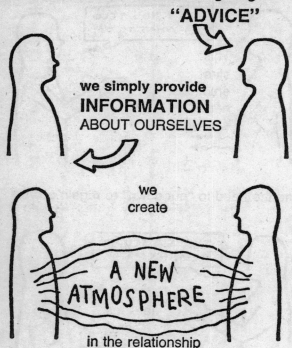

we simply provide
INFORMATION
ABOUT OURSELVES

we
create

A NEW
ATMOSPHERE

in the relationship
because
"ADVICE" says "YOU ARE A **CHILD**"
("You aren't capable of leading your own life")
while
"INFORMATION" says "YOU ARE AN **ADULT**"
("I respect your right to choose what you do
based on the information I give you")

152

While hearing **ADVICE** . . .

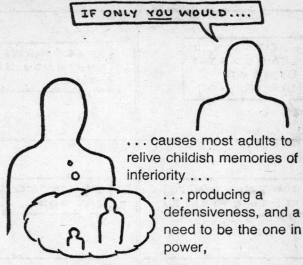

IF ONLY <u>YOU</u> WOULD....

. . . causes most adults to relive childish memories of inferiority . . .

. . . producing a defensiveness, and a need to be the one in power,

when only **INFORMATION** is given

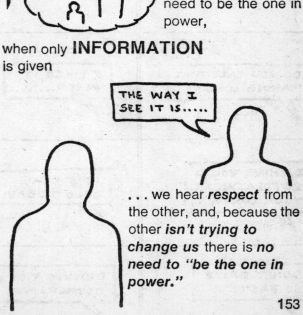

THE WAY I SEE IT IS.....

. . . we hear *respect* from the other, and, because the other *isn't trying to change us* there is *no need to "be the one in power."*

Examples of **ADVICE** are:	Examples of **INFORMATION** are:
WHEN ARE YOU GOING TO STOP BEING SO IRRITATING?	I GET IRRITATED WHEN YOU DO THAT.
DON'T YOU REALIZE IT'S TIME TO EAT?	I'D LIKE TO EAT SOON.
DO YOU CALL THAT MAKING LOVE?	I LIKED IT WHEN.......
I THINK YOU'D BETTER WEAR YOUR COAT!	IT'S VERY COLD TODAY
DON'T DRIVE SO FAST!	DRIVING THIS FAST BOTHERS ME!

It is important to be aware that information
does not always have to be quietly dignified:

If we have listened with understanding
OVER AN EXTENDED PERIOD OF TIME
and have become increasingly frustrated,
if we quietly state

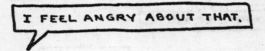

the other person may not
believe that what we are saying is true, and,
(with good reason), question our honesty in
other matters as well.

is ultimately far more helpful because it is *real*
... but it is still *information*, *not advice*.

In the "telephone" situation mentioned previously, defining our territory might result in a conversation such as this:

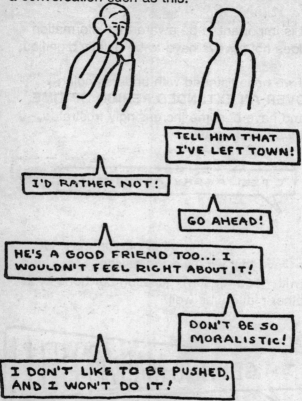

NOTE that in this comment the person is simply *stating his own position*, but not attacking the other person with a cutting remark (such as "At least I'm not a hypocrite like *you* are!").

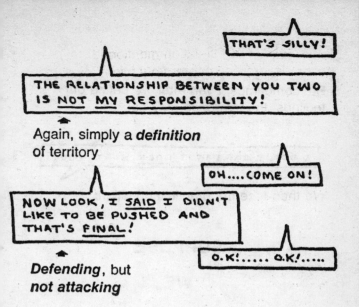

Again, simply a *definition*
of territory

Defending, but
not attacking

While responses
such as these
may temporarily strain the relationship, the
honesty of the response generally promotes
mutual respect.

At times, such directness may even *deepen*
a friendship.

> I KNOW YOU'LL GIVE ME A STRAIGHT
> ANSWER. WHAT'S YOUR OPINION OF
> MY RELATIONSHIP WITH HIM?

When one person is quietly "giving in" there
is no **REAL** friendship anyway, only a
superficial relationship.

157

But sometimes, even after we define our feelings, the response may be:

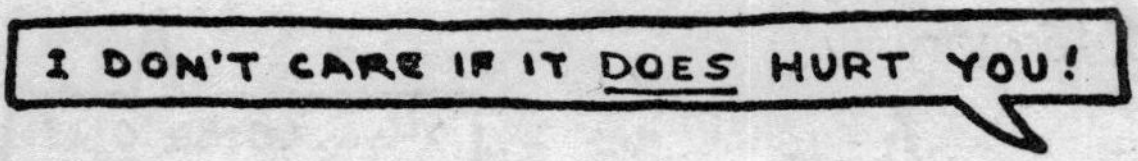

I DON'T CARE IF IT DOES HURT YOU!

We then face the practical question:

SUPPOSE

WE

DEFINE

OUR

"OUCH!" LINE

AND

IT'S

NOT RESPECTED?

We then **D E F E N D** ourselves

by

*Quietly stating what
we will do* under
various circumstances:

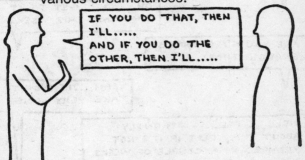

> IF YOU DO THAT, THEN
> I'LL.....
> AND IF YOU DO THE
> OTHER, THEN I'LL.....

This is **NOT A THREAT ...**

> IF YOU DON'T <u>SHAPE UP</u>, I'LL.....

NOR WHINING ...

> WHY CAN'T YOU <u>HELP ME</u>?......

BUT INFORMATION about ourselves:

> I'M SORRY, BUT I <u>HAVE</u> TO DO THIS
> FOR MY OWN <u>SELF RESPECT</u>.

An example of "defending":

I'M GETTING VERY FRUSTRATED TRYING TO USE THAT WHEN IT'S BROKEN.

I TOLD YOU I'D FIX IT.

I KNOW....BUT WHEN?

OH.....I'LL GET TO IT SOMETIME THIS WEEK.

ARE YOU SURE THAT'S ENOUGH TIME?

YEAH.....IT WON'T TAKE VERY LONG.

WELL, I FEEL SO STRONGLY ABOUT THIS, THAT IF IT'S NOT REPAIRED IN A COUPLE OF WEEKS I'M GOING TO <u>HIRE</u> SOMEONE TO DO IT.

Note that this is *not a threat* – "If you *don't,* I'll get someone who *will!"* – but rather a quiet expression of SELF RESPECT.

DEFENDING ourselves

also means

TAKING
APPROPRIATE
ACTION

. . . demonstrating responsibility
by acting on what we said
we would do.

> I HIRED SOMEONE TODAY
> TO MAKE THOSE REPAIRS.

> ARE YOU OUT OF YOUR MIND?
> I TOLD YOU A COUPLE OF WEEKS
> AGO THAT I WOULD DO IT.!!

> I KNOW YOU WANT TO FIX
> IT, BUT I RESPECT MYSELF
> TOO MUCH TO USE IT ANY
> LONGER WHEN IT'S BROKEN.

This is not an attack,
but simply "protection
of territory."

161

Sometimes our territory may have become so small, by consistently "giving in," that there is little left.

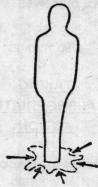

When we have allowed this to happen, we find that we are "taken for granted," and eventually become resentful.

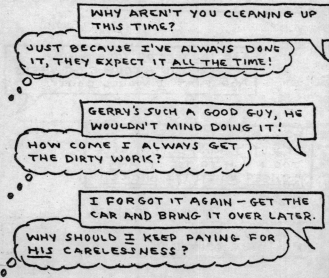

Usually it is easier for ourselves and others if territory that has been given up is regained *gradually*.

It is helpful to start reclaiming our territory in a *relatively small area.*

Such an approach slowly builds confidence in our own self worth. Reclaiming territory *will* anger others who "don't expect that" from us. (But we must be prepared to face such anger; after all we did allow it to happen!) . . . however, doing it *gradually* gives time for everyone (including ourselves) to adjust to the new situation.

Regaining our *selves* comes about through phrases such as these:

IT'S SOMEONE ELSE'S TURN TO CLEAN UP.

I WOULD MIND DOING THAT.

I'VE DECIDED THAT IF YOU FORGET IT AGAIN, YOU'LL HAVE TO GET IT YOURSELF.

163

In Summary, then
HAVING THE COURAGE TO BE
means
DEFINING and DEFENDING
our territory . . .
NOT TELLING THE OTHER
WHAT HE SHOULD DO:

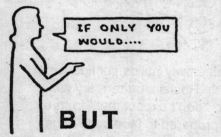

IF ONLY YOU WOULD....

BUT

1. MAKING OUR
   EMOTIONS KNOWN

I FEEL....

2. QUIETLY
   INFORMING THE
   OTHER OF OUR
   PLAN OF ACTION

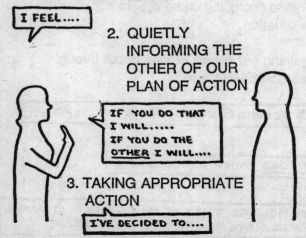

IF YOU DO THAT
I WILL.....
IF YOU DO THE
OTHER I WILL....

3. TAKING APPROPRIATE
   ACTION

I'VE DECIDED TO....

Paradoxically . . .

LOVING OURSELVES

FREES US TO LOVE OTHERS — AND MAKES IT EASIER FOR OTHERS TO LOVE US.

When we do *not* take responsibility for our own self (by defining and defending our territory) we feel a "lack of love" and may turn to manipulating others to get the love we "deserve."

On the other hand, when we take responsibility for our own needs then the other person no longer feels obligated to help, and can experience real joy in giving. Freedom to give makes love possible.

Loving ourselves frees us to love others — and makes it easier for others to love us . . .

because . . .

LOVE IS WHAT HAPPENS WHEN THERE IS FREEDOM FROM SELF CONCERN

CHAPTER VI

EXPLORING ALTERNATIVES

We also act creatively in
a "power" situation
when we

4

EXPLORE
ALTERNATIVES
WITH
SELF
RESPECT

"EXPLORING ALTERNATIVES WITH 'SELF' RESPECT"

MEANS

SORTING THROUGH

VARIOUS SOLUTIONS

TRYING TO

DISCOVER

Most struggles center around
"A PROBLEM"

and the

MEANING

that the solution has for each person.

For example ...

IF

MEANS
be-ing hurt
then **"protecting ourselves"** will claim all
our attention and we are not free
to look elsewhere — to **"explore alternatives
with self respect."**

In exploring how our *framework of* MEANING affects relationships, consider how our *viewpoint* determines what is seen in this illustration.

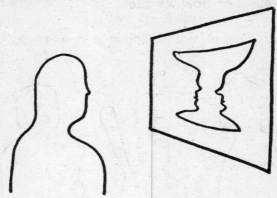

If it is seen as a "vase" then the details of the outline have a certain meaning, (the contours of the vase) . . .

. . . but if the **meaning** we bring to the picture is "two faces in profile" then the details of those same lines are seen quite differently.

The **meaning** we bring to every situation has an effect on **how we see:**

If three people are looking at an open field . . .

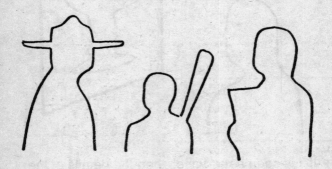

| and this person is a farmer | and this person is a boy with a new baseball bat | and this person is a building contractor |

each will see that same field in a somewhat different way. The framework of MEANING determines the details.

The over-all meaning we give to a relationship determines our actions.

If the relationship
MEANS

"PROTECTING OURSELVES"

our words and actions
will "fit in" with that
meaning:

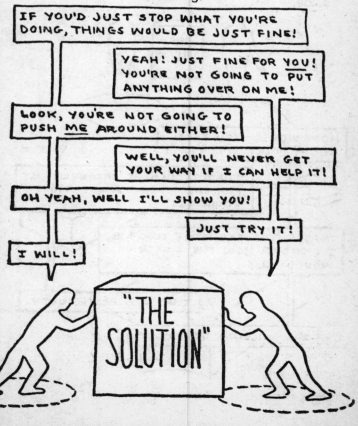

On the other hand,
   If the relationship
      MEANS

"EXPLORING ALTERNATIVES WITH SELF RESPECT"

then our words and actions will "fit in" with *that* meaning, and the problem solutions can be set aside.

Our minds work in such a way that *we cannot bring* TWO MEANINGS *to something* AT THE SAME TIME.

either we see the "vase" **or** the "FACES" — but **not both at the same moment.**

In the illustration it is a relatively simple matter to change the over-all viewpoint and give an entirely different meaning to the details.

In human relationships, however to change the over-all viewpoint is far more difficult.

Because we cannot give TWO MEANINGS
to something at the same time, when
strong emotions are present, it's
almost impossible to change the
focus of meaning
from
"EMOTION" to **"LOGIC"**
because
we must choose **either** one **or**
the other, and emotions have a
stronger claim on our attention

Yet when **EITHER** person

DEMONSTRATES THAT HE CARES by
choosing the priority of emotional
understanding over "facts" by

TRUSTING

   LISTENING

      CLARIFYING

then it becomes easier *to change the focus
of attention to another "framework of
meaning."*

BUT — alternative
solutions ("FACTS") can be
explored only

AFTER

**EMOTIONS HAVE BEEN UNDERSTOOD,
AND THAT UNDERSTANDING MADE
CLEAR.**

We keep moving toward a solution when we *focus on exploring alternatives* with "self" respect, and *keep information moving back and forth* between us.

Sometimes when information is being exchanged *emotional problems arise which cloud the free exchange of information.*

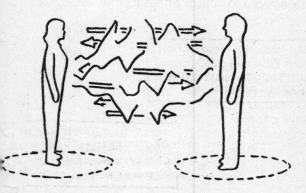

At such a point it is necessary to return, (perhaps again and again), to focusing on the emotions . . . trusting . . . listening . . . clarifying . . . before continuing with the "facts."

Once the emotions have been "heard," it will be possible to return again to the "facts" . . .

The following questions will help maintain a focus, while moving toward a solution.

Answers to some of the questions will be quite obvious, others may require considerable thought. It depends on the specific problem.

Rather than work through each question in detail, it will be useful to use the questions as a **CHECK LIST***

---

1. *What* specifically is to be solved?
2. *When* must it be solved?
3. Is it possible to *expand the time available* before a final decision must be made?
4. What are the *limits* within which we must work — those things that probably won't change? (Could any of these limits be changed, though costly?)
5. Has the main *meaning* of the problem *for each person* been made clear?
6. Has holding on to a *particular solution* become more important than what needs to be done?
7. What *resources* are available to solve the problem?
8. Am I remaining open to a *new and unfamiliar solution* to the problem?
9. What is the *next step?*
10. Am I using my *emotions* to continually, test the solution being considered?

SUMMARY OF STEPS TO BE TAKEN IN MOVING FROM A POWER STRUGGLE TO A CREATIVE RELATIONSHIP

It is important to be aware that each step does not automatically lead to the next. In the process of moving toward a creative relationship, it may be necessary to return and repeat previous steps before continuing.

1. *Realizing* that all emotions are acceptable (but not all actions).
2. *Trusting* — Making a conscious effort to withhold judgment (not "pushing" our own viewpoint).
3. *Listening* — Trying to hear the other's emotional viewpoint.
4. *Clarifying* — Demonstrating our willingness to listen by making clear what feelings have been heard before discussing "facts."
5. *Defining* — Clarifying our own territory by making emotions known.
6. *Defending* — Protecting our territory, by quietly stating choices and taking appropriate action.
7. *Exploring Alternatives* — Examining other solutions with self respect.

Risking – Being willing to face change

In contrast to most of the steps above which generally move from one to the other in the order listed, "risking" is a part of the process and is usually helpful at any point.

AFTERWORD

RISKING CHANGE

Usually if the preceding steps are followed the relationship will greatly improve. Sometimes, however, relationships are such that this does not happen.

**WHAT, THEN,
CAN BE DONE
IF THERE IS
NOT MUCH
CHANGE IN THE
RELATIONSHIP?**

In such a situation, we
may have to

5

RISK

A CHANGE

IN OUR

OWN

POSITION

Often we are kept from acting creatively
because we feel comfortable with that which is

FAMILIAR

Understandably, all of us find that

THE FAMILIAR
MEANS SECURITY

and that which is

STRANGE or DIFFERENT
MEANS
INSECURITY

Yet . . .

GROWTH

INVOLVES

RISK

"An essential aspect of creativity is not being
afraid to fail."

— Edwin Land

1. Often there is no change because we are not willing to **RISK** seeing **OURSELVES as we are.**

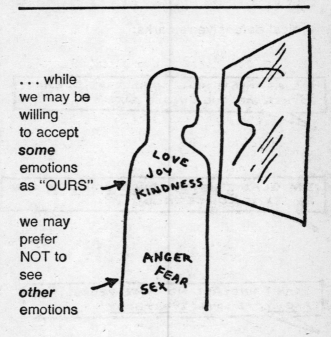

... while we may be willing to accept *some* emotions as "OURS" →

LOVE
JOY
KINDNESS

we may prefer NOT to see *other* emotions →

ANGER
FEAR
SEX

... because it seems that having those emotions means we are "bad" or "unacceptable."

When we try to hide our emotions from ourselves, others see our defensiveness and are less trustful of the relationship

typical defensive remarks:

ME AFRAID? HEH...HEH...THAT DOESN'T BOTHER ME ONE SINGLE BIT!

I'M GLAD I HAVE A PURE MIND AS FAR AS SEX IS CONCERNED!

I CAN'T UNDERSTAND WHY PEOPLE GET ANGRY. I LOVE EVERYBODY!

Sometimes it is possible to deny our feelings so continually that we no longer have conscious awareness of certain emotions.

188

However, when we accept ourselves as we are, our relationships with others change because we have an "openness" that puts others at ease

typical "open" remarks:

> I GUESS I REALLY AM THAT WAY, AND I'D BETTER FACE IT!

> I SEE NOW THAT I REALLY DIDN'T MEAN THAT. I JUST SAID IT SO SHE'D LIKE ME.

> THIS SITUATION IS REALLY GETTING ME UP TIGHT. I CAN FEEL IT IN MY STOMACH!

and sometimes we may hear the reply:

> YOU KNOW....I FEEL THE SAME WAY!

2. Another reason that change may not occur is that we may not be willing to **RISK** the **other person's seeing us as we are.**

If we set up a phony image of ourselves to relate to, the other person cannot know who we really "are"

... and we actually communicate "I want your cooperation, but I don't trust you enough to let you know who I am."

We hide ourselves behind remarks such as . . .

A real relationship only becomes possible when we are willing to reveal our emotions to another.

Unfortunately, *rather than risk rejection* we may settle for a relationship

that

is

PHONY IMAGE TO PHONY IMAGE

... when it is possible to have a creative relationship

that

is

PERSON TO PERSON

"If you *forfeit* the game, you *don't lose*, but you *don't WIN either!*"
— Richard L. Johnson

3. Sometimes when the *other person* will *not cooperate* it may be necessary to **RISK** a **change in the relationship itself.**

In understanding what this means it might be helpful to visualize a relationship as like being on a see-saw with another person:

When we see that the relationship is "out-of-balance" our tendency is to point our finger at the other and tell him or her . . .

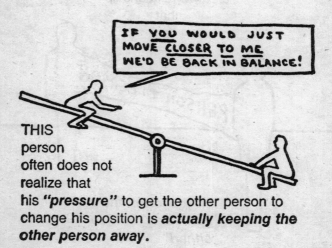

IF YOU WOULD JUST MOVE CLOSER TO ME WE'D BE BACK IN BALANCE!

THIS person often does not realize that his *"pressure"* to get the other person to change his position is *actually keeping the other person away.*

"PRESSURE" on the other person in an attempt to "get love" is seen in phrases like these . . .

YOU NEVER PAY ANY ATTENTION TO WHAT I DO!

DON'T MY TEARS MEAN ANYTHING TO YOU?

YOU'RE MY WHOLE LIFE! WITHOUT YOU IT'S NOTHING!

WHY CAN'T YOU SHOW SOME APPRECIATION FOR MY WORK?

WHY CAN'T YOU BE MORE AFFECTIONATE?

YOU NEVER SPEND ANY TIME WITH ME!

A change in the "balance" of the relationship
may also occur
if
this
person ...

**↓ *feels good enough
about himself to
risk "not being close"***
and
backs   away

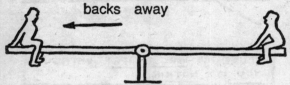

typical "risking" statements:

I HAVE TOO MUCH SELF RESPECT TO
KEEP TAKING THAT ANYMORE.

I'M <u>VERY</u> ANGRY WITH YOU.

I'VE DECIDED THAT IT'S BEST
TO BE APART FOR A WHILE.

and ...

I'M FED UP WITH YOUR PUSHING ME AROUND.

IT'S TOO PAINFUL FOR ME TO CONTINUE THIS RELATIONSHIP.

. . . all are phrases of **self respect**.

Such "risking the relationship" has a "freeing" effect on the other person, because he no longer has to ask, ***"How can I deal with this pressure?*** but is free to ask, "What do I **want** to do about this **relationship**?"

OFTEN when pressure has been removed, the person who has been pressured will, of his own accord, move closer again.

197

To "RISK THE RELATIONSHIP ITSELF" means an *actual risk* rather than a "bluff" or a "threat" to manipulate the other person.

A "bluff" or a "threat" is destructive rather than helpful, because manipulation of another means a lack of respect and love.

It neither provides

> **"Conditions that make it
> easy for the other person to
> BE who he is"**

... nor does it include

> **"The courage to
> BE ourselves"**

Although "risking may ultimately make things worse rather than better, it is usually better than living continuously with pain, and with "what if . . ."

We learn by making choices.

198

Some relationships, however, may reach the point where, if they continue, one or the other's "self" will continually be hurt.

To risk a relationship may mean that the best solution is to leave the relationship and go elsewhere (another job, marriage, friend, etc.).

A complete break in a relationship is usually not necessary, however. Standing up for one's self may simply mean a break in the "old" type of relationship, and accepting a "new" relationship with the same person ("a re-negotiation of the 'contract' ").

199

While we must face the fact that

NOT ALL PROBLEMS
CAN BE
"SOLVED"

No matter what the conditions are,

it is always possible to

IMPROVE THE SITUATION

when
we are willing
for others,
and ourselves,
to
"BE"

APPENDIX A

SUMMARY EXAMPLES
#1. IN A HOME
#2. AT WORK

SUMMARY EXAMPLE #1 IN A HOME

> WELL, I SEE YOU'VE MADE A MESS OF THINGS, AS USUAL!

1. *Realizing all emotions are acceptable* (but not all actions).

> OH...HE'S REALLY BUGGING ME TODAY! THAT CONSTANT CRITICISM IS TOO MUCH! ...I <u>HATE</u> HIM FOR THAT!.... WHAT'S THE <u>MATTER</u> WITH <u>ME</u>?....I MUST BE AN AWFUL PERSON TO HAVE THAT ANGER.....<u>NO</u>, THAT'S NOT TRUE, <u>ANY</u> FEELING I HAVE IS O.K.! IT'S THERE FOR A PURPOSE...BUT I DON'T HAVE TO ACT ON IT...

2. *Trusting – Making a conscious effort to withhold judgment* (not "pushing" our own viewpoint).

> I'D STILL LIKE TO TELL HIM OFF, THOUGH! IT'S INCREDIBLE HOW I ALWAYS GET THE BLAME...I CAN'T UNDERSTAND HIS ATTITUDE!....WELL, KNOWING HOW HIS MOTHER PUSHED HIM AROUND, MAYBE I CAN UNDERSTAND PART OF IT....I'M STILL TEMPTED TO "PUSH" BACK, BUT THAT WON'T HELP EITHER OF US.... I'D BETTER LISTEN....

> I DON'T UNDERSTAND WHAT YOU MEAN....

> NATURALLY! YOU'RE SO STUPID, YOU'RE JUST LIKE ALL WOMEN, YOU NEVER UNDERSTAND ANYTHING! ...YOU DIDN'T SEND THE MONEY FOR THE VACATION COTTAGE, LIKE I TOLD YOU TO DO! GET IT?!!

3. *Listening — trying to hear the other's emotional viewpoint.*

> WHEEEW! I HEAR HIM LOUD AND CLEAR! HE'S FURIOUS ABOUT MY NOT SENDING THAT MONEY!

4. *Clarifying — Demonstrating our willingness to hear by making clear what feelings have been heard before discussing "facts".*

> EXPLAINING WON'T HELP NOW! FIRST HE'S GOT TO KNOW THAT I CARE ENOUGH ABOUT OUR RELATIONSHIP TO HEAR WHAT HE IS SAYING...."DESCRIBE HIS FEELINGS IN MY OWN WORDS."....HE'S MADE ME SO ANGRY IT'S NOT EASY....BUT HERE GOES....

204

I HEAR YOU SAYING THAT YOU'RE ANGRY WITH ME FOR NOT SENDING THAT RENT MONEY FOR THE COTTAGE!

IT'S NICE TO KNOW THAT YOU HEAR SOMETHING, YOU NEVER DO!

YOU FEEL I NEVER LISTEN TO ANYTHING YOU SAY!

YOU SURE DON'T!

YOU'RE SAYING I NEVER HEAR YOU!

A slight softening ➤ of the anger

YOU SURE DON'T!...WELL MOST OF THE TIME YOU DON'T.... ALMOST NEVER!

YOU FEEL I DON'T HEAR YOU MOST OF THE TIME!

YES!!

At this point the emotional pressure is not as strong as it was, but confirmation of willingness to hear must continue *until the person attacking knows that his emotional viewpoint has been heard.*

> YOU FEEL I'M LIVING IN MY OWN LITTLE DREAM WORLD, AND NOT VERY AWARE OF WHAT'S GOING ON WITH YOU!

> THAT'S <u>JUST</u> THE WAY I FEEL!

The process of trusting, listening, and clarifying must continue until emotional pressure has been reduced to the point where clarification of territory can be discussed.

> I'VE LISTENED TO YOU, NOW I'D LIKE TO TELL YOU HOW I FEEL.

> GO AHEAD!

5. *Defining — Clarifying our own territory by making our emotions known.*

> <u>WELL</u>....? WHY DIDN'T YOU SEND THE MONEY FOR THE COTTAGE?

> I DIDN'T WANT TO GO THERE AGAIN THIS YEAR. THAT'S <u>NOT</u> A VACATION FOR <u>ME</u>. IT'S MORE WORK THAN STAYING HOME!

206

Defining territory often leads to a further attack, and, if it is intense, previous steps in listening may again have to be repeated.

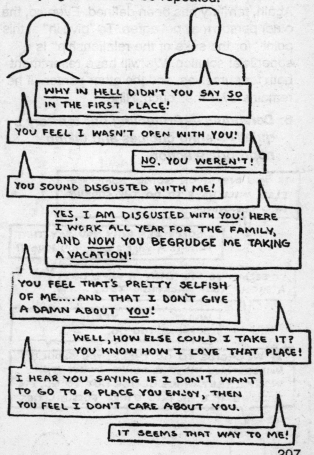

207

> I KNOW YOU WORK HARD, AND I WANT
> YOU TO ENJOY YOUR VACATION. I
> JUST DON'T WANT TO SPEND THAT
> TIME WORKING.

Again, territory has been defined. Even so, the other person may not agree. To "give in" at this point "for the sake of the relationship" is a superficial solution. We will have resentment both for ourselves, and the other person, if he remains over the "ouch!" line.

6. *Defending — Protecting our territory by quietly stating choices and taking appropriate action.*

> IF YOU INSIST ON GOING, SOMEONE
> ELSE WILL HAVE TO DO THE COOKING
> AND CLEANING.

> I DON'T SEE WHY YOU SAY THAT.
> THAT IS A WIFE'S JOB, YOU KNOW!

> IT SEEMS TO ME THAT A WIFE HAS
> A RIGHT TO A VACATION TOO.

> WELL...........YEAH.............I
> SUPPOSE YOU DO.

> IF WE DECIDE TO GO THERE, YOU SHOULD
> UNDERSTAND THAT I DON'T WANT TO
> WORK.....BUT IF WE DECIDE NOT TO GO, I'M
> WILLING TO LOOK INTO OTHER POSSIBILITIES.

208

Before the problem is resolved, still other situations may arise which necessitate listening on the part of the **other** person before going further — reversing the previous roles of speaker and listener.

For example, the couple might go to bed before the problem has been solved:

> DON'T TOUCH ME! HOW DO YOU EXPECT ME TO MAKE LOVE AFTER THE WAY YOU TREATED ME TODAY?

> YOU FEEL THAT I WAS UNFAIR THIS AFTERNOON, AND YOU'RE STILL VERY ANGRY ABOUT IT.

> AFTER WHAT HAPPENED, YOU CAN'T EXPECT ME TO JUST FLIP A SWITCH AND TURN ON THE AFFECTION!

> YOU'RE SAYING THAT YOU CAN'T CHANGE YOUR EMOTIONS THAT QUICKLY.

> I FEEL YOU'RE JUST USING ME.

> YOU CAN'T UNDERSTAND HOW I COULD REALLY CARE ABOUT YOU AFTER THE THINGS I SAID...AND YOU FEEL USED.

IT'S HARD TO BELIEVE THAT YOU LOVE ME AFTER THE WAY YOU PUT ME DOWN!

◀ It's tempting for the listener to want to "comment" or "explain" here, but the person is not ready to hear. Further confirmation of feelings are needed first.

IT MAKES YOU QUESTION MY SINCERITY....

WELL...HOW ELSE COULD I FEEL? IT'S PRETTY OBVIOUS, ISN'T IT?

YOU FEEL IT'S OBVIOUS THAT I DON'T LOVE YOU AT ALL.

WELL, I KNOW YOU CARE SOMETIMES, BUT YOU HURT ME VERY DEEPLY TODAY.

◀ The anger softens a little here

IT WAS PAINFUL FOR YOU... HUH?

YES...

The intensity of the emotion here is so great that it will not be resolved without a great deal more listening . . . Even in this brief exchange however, the beginning of a change of mood can be seen.

7. *Exploring Alternatives — Examining other solutions with self respect.*
And the next day when discussion resumes . . .

> I DON'T FEEL ANY DIFFERENTLY TODAY ABOUT WHAT I SAID YESTERDAY. I STILL DON'T WANT TO SPEND VACATION TIME WORKING IN THE COTTAGE.

> I'VE BEEN THINKING ABOUT IT, AND I CAN UNDERSTAND HOW YOU WOULD FEEL THAT WAY. BUT HOW WAS I TO KNOW THAT IT BOTHERED YOU....YOU NEVER SAID ANYTHING ABOUT IT BEFORE THIS.

> IT'S BOTHERED ME FOR YEARS. I GUESS I SHOULD HAVE TOLD YOU LONG BEFORE THIS.

Yes! Defining the place of the "ouch!" line is the responsibility of the person *within* it.

> I WONDER IF WE COULD WORK OUT SOMETHING THAT WOULD BE O.K. WITH US BOTH.

> LIKE WHAT?

WELL, HOW ABOUT EATING ALL OUR MEALS IN THAT RESTAURANT IN TOWN?

THAT'S SO EXPENSIVE I <u>COULDN'T</u> ENJOY IT AND <u>NEITHER</u> WOULD <u>YOU!</u>

◀ It's helpful for her to define her "ouch!" line.
◀ Unfortunately she goes on and defines *his* too.

When we define another's territory the person may become irritated and not know quite why. Actually it brings back the childhood feeling of "You have to be told for your own good." It is subtly giving "advice" rather than "information."

He's somewhat bothered, but still open to "exploring alternatives" ➡

IF I DIDN'T WANT TO DO IT I WOULDN'T HAVE SUGGESTED IT ......DO YOU HAVE A <u>BETTER</u> IDEA?

HOW ABOUT GOING TO TURTLEBACK LODGE?

A definition of his territory ➡

NO....I WANT TO GO TO A PLACE WHERE I CAN FISH.

Using the problem check list (page 181) might be useful at this point.

A Problem Check List

1. **What**, specifically, is to be solved?

   We both want an enjoyable and restful vacation.

2. **When** must it be solved?

   Within the month.

3. Is it possible to **expand the time available** before a final decision must be made?

   Not necessary.

4. What are the **limits** within which we must work? (Could any of these limits be changed, though costly?)

   Little or no housework.
   Fishing available.
   Can't spend more than $500.

5. Has the main **meaning** of the problem **for each person been made clear?**

   Yes.

6. Has holding on to a *particular solution* become more important than what needs to be done?

    Maybe.

7. What *resources* are available to solve the problem?

    Friends.
    Travel Agency.

8. Is there openness to a *new and unfamiliar solution* to the problem?

    A vacation with some housework and without fishing would be considered if it is enjoyable and restful for both.

9. What is the *next step?*

    Check with friends and travel agency to explore other possibilities.

10. Is each person continually using his *emotions* to test the solution being considered?

    So far O.K. - to be rechecked later.

214

WELL, WHAT DID YOU FIND OUT ABOUT THE VACATION POSSIBILITIES?

I ASKED A LOT OF PEOPLE BUT NOTHING SOUNDED VERY GOOD TO ME..... WHAT ABOUT YOU?

MOST OF THE FRIENDS I TALKED WITH GO TO THE SAME PLACE EACH YEAR JUST AS WE DO............... AND THEN I GOT TO THINKING......... WHY DON'T WE DO SOMETHING ENTIRELY DIFFERENT THIS YEAR?

FOR INSTANCE?

Risking — Being willing to face change.

..........WELL........I'VE BEEN THINKING ABOUT THE JOHNSONS. THEY APPRECIATED BEING OUR GUESTS AT THE COTTAGE BEFORE THEY MOVED.......AND THEY'VE BEEN BEGGING US TO VISIT THEM IN THEIR NEW HOME.........

YEAH?....?

.........I'M AFRAID YOU'RE GOING TO LAUGH AT ME, OR BE ANGRY..........BUT.....WELL.. ...I CHECKED INTO IT.....AND WE COULD FLY THERE AND BACK FOR $250.......AND WE HAVEN'T SEEN THEM FOR A WHILE.....

WELL, IT IS A PRETTY CRAZY IDEA TO GO WAY OUT THERE FOR A VACATION...........
....BUT.......WELL...........MAYBE IT'S NOT SO CRAZY AFTER ALL..........

I PHONED THEM TO SEE IF IT WOULD BE CONVENIENT, AND <u>IF</u> WE DECIDE TO GO, IT'S FINE WITH THEM.....WE COULD EVEN SPEND SOME TIME ON OUR OWN......IT'S OFF SEASON RATES, AND I WOULDN'T MIND GETTING A ROOM WITH A KITCHEN FOR PART OF THE TIME......AND YOU'D GET A CHANCE TO TRY DEEP SEA FISHING.

....YEAH......HMMM......YEAH........ ....IT SOUNDS PRETTY GOOD.....

While this example may seem simple or superficial, the basic principles seen here apply in a wide variety of situations. Their true validity, however will only be understood through trial and error in life situations.

> I'M GLAD YOU'RE COMING TO WORK FOR US. I'VE ALWAYS BELIEVED THAT A PERSON SHOULD BE HIRED BECAUSE OF HIS ABILITY, AND NOT BY THE COLOR OF HIS SKIN, OR HIS RACE. IT DOESN'T BOTHER ME AT ALL! NOT A BIT! NOT A BIT!

> UH! OH!

> YES SIR! I'M GLAD YOU'RE HERE! I BELIEVE IN PROMOTING BROTHERHOOD!

1 *Realizing all emotions are acceptable.*

> HERE I AM AT A NEW JOB, AND INSTEAD OF BEING GLAD, I'M ANGRY!...I SHOULDN'T FEEL THIS WAY....NO, DAMN IT!... I DO FEEL THIS WAY.... SOMEPLACE IN ME THIS ANGER MAKES SENSE.....AND IT'S ALL RIGHT FOR ME TO HAVE THESE FEELINGS!

2. *Trusting — making a conscious effort to withhold judgment.*

> YOU AND YOUR SUPERIOR ATTITUDE!
> IF YOU'D JUST BE HONEST ABOUT THE
> WAY YOU FEEL, IT WOULD BE A LOT
> EASIER!.....I DON'T THINK YOU EVEN
> SEE YOUR OWN PREJUDICE.....I'VE GOT
> TO REMEMBER THAT!.....HE MAY NOT
> REALLY KNOW WHAT HE'S DOING.....
> THAT'S HARD TO BELIEVE....BUT I
> GUESS I CAN AT LEAST WAIT AND SEE!

> YEAH, I REALLY WANT TO HELP
> YOU PEOPLE!

3. *Listening — Trying to hear the other's emotional viewpoint.*

> I THINK HE REALLY BELIEVES THAT
> HIMSELF — THAT HE'S TRYING TO BE
> HELPFUL....HE MAY BE SINCERE,
> EVEN IF HE IS INSENSITIVE....I'LL
> TELL HIM WHAT I HEAR HIM SAYING...

4. *Clarifying — Demonstrating our willingness to hear by making clear what feelings have been heard before discussing "facts."*

I HEAR YOU SAYING THAT YOU WANT TO HELP PEOPLE LIKE ME

IS *THAT* WHAT I SAID?

DID *I REALLY* SAY THAT?....
I GUESS I DID....HE MUST THINK
I'M AWFULLY ARROGANT....THIS
SITUATION IS MAKING ME ANXIOUS
....I WANT IT TO GO WELL....I CAN
TELL HE'S ANXIOUS TOO, EVEN
THOUGH I HARDLY KNOW HIM....
WE SHOULDN'T FEEL THIS WAY....
WHAT DO I MEAN WE *SHOULDN'T*
FEEL THIS WAY? WE *DO*....AT LEAST
I DO, AND I'D BETTER ACCEPT IT

An attempt to accept *his* emotions.

I THOUGHT THAT'S WHAT YOU SAID.

I GUESS THAT SOUNDED PRETTY
ARROGANT. MAYBE WE'RE BOTH
A LITTLE UP TIGHT.

I GUESS WE *ARE* BOTH A LITTLE UNEASY!

MAYBE HE REALLY HAS SOME
SENSITIVITY AFTER ALL.

Even in a situation in which each person is
consciously trying to promote a good
relationship, inevitably conditions will arise in
which the two people disagree. When
disagreement occurs, childhood emotions, and
ways of relating, may come to the surface and
center around a particular issue The intensity
of these emotions may become far greater
than is appropriate to the actual problem.

I'M SORRY, BUT YOU'LL HAVE
TO STAY LATE TONIGHT TO
FINISH THAT WORK.

WHY DIDN'T YOU TELL ME
BEFORE NOW? I HAVE AN
APPOINTMENT WITH SOMEONE
IN 45 MINUTES, AND THE
PERSON HAS ALREADY LEFT
TO MEET ME.

I TOLD YOU THAT YOU MIGHT
HAVE TO WORK LATE SOMETIMES.
WE CAN'T RUN OUR BUSINESS
AROUND YOUR SOCIAL LIFE.

While this sounds like "information," it is really
an attack. The speaker infers "you're
irresponsible," yet nothing has been said to
indicate this.

SUMMARY EXAMPLE # 2
(continued)

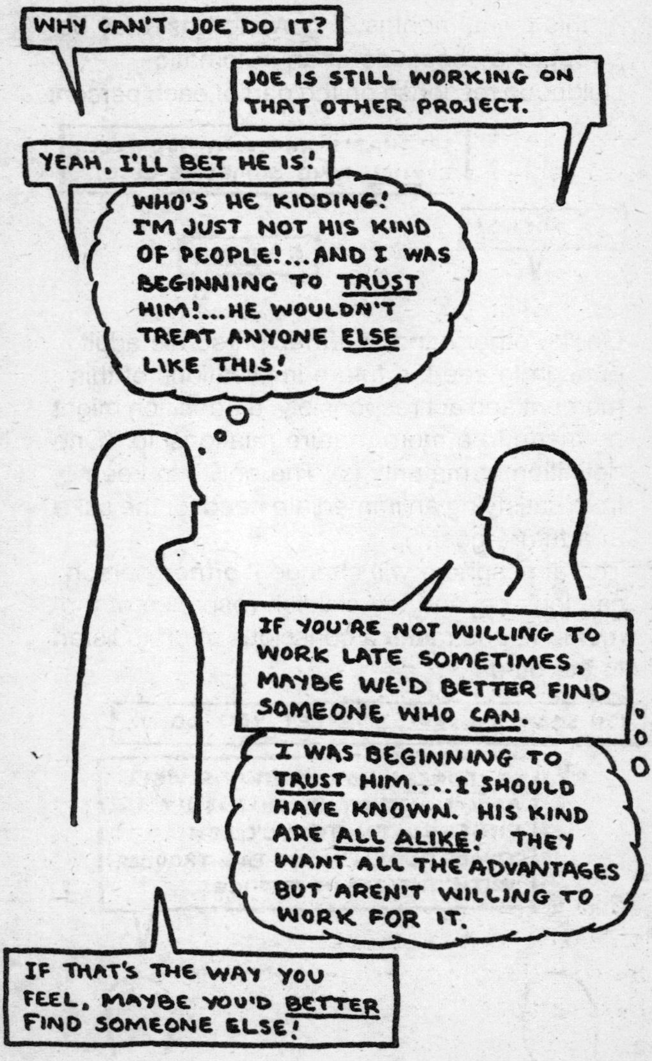

At this point, months of growing trust may be swept away because of an automatic childhood response on the part of each person.

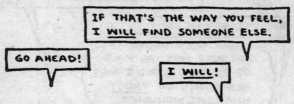

On the other hand, if *either* person is adult enough to see the future implications of this moment and act responsibly, a transition might be made to a more mature relationship. (One definition of maturity is "The ability to keep from satisfying an immediate need for the sake of a future goal.")

The atmosphere will change if *either* person can look beyond the childish response of the moment, and make a conscious effort to listen to the other.

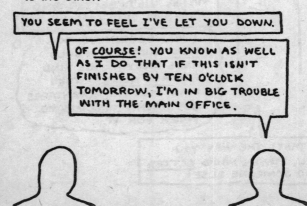

YOU FEEL I SHOULD HAVE KNOWN HOW IMPORTANT THIS WAS TO YOU, AND PLANNED TO STAY LATE TONIGHT.

YOU'VE GOT TO LEARN THAT WHEN YOU HAVE A JOB LIKE THIS, YOU'VE GOT TO TAKE RESPONSIBILITY.

He's coming on as a "parent" here.

I HEAR YOU SAYING THAT I HAVEN'T LEARNED TO TAKE RESPONSIBILITY.

WELL......NOT ENTIRELY...I JUST CAN'T <u>BELIEVE</u> YOU'D <u>DO</u> THIS TO ME!

YOU THOUGHT YOU COULD TRUST ME, AND NOW IT SEEMS YOU CAN'T.

YES!

While the problem is far from solved, the atmosphere has already begun to change ... preparing the way for a relationship where a solution may be possible, but more listening would still be helpful. The listener too has a need to be heard, and a better solution is possible if he can know that his emotions are also understood before going further.

223

Which person listens first is rather unimportant. A similar improvement in the relationship would also occur if listening began with the other person

> YOU FEEL THAT I'M BEING UNFAIR TO YOU?

> YES! YOU DIDN'T SAY ANYTHING TO ME ABOUT STAYING LATE UNTIL <u>NOW</u>!

> YOU FEEL THAT IF I WANTED YOU TO STAY LATE, I SHOULD HAVE TOLD YOU BEFORE THIS.

> WELL, YOU <u>DO</u> LET OTHER PEOPLE KNOW AHEAD OF TIME.

He's saying in a gentle way what bothers him most — that he's not being respected for himself.

> YOU FEEL THAT YOU'RE BEING TREATED DIFFERENTLY THAN OTHERS AROUND HERE.

> YES! AND <u>YOU</u> <u>KNOW</u> <u>IT</u> AS WELL AS I DO!

The most common response of a listener at this point is to "explain," but more listening first will be far more helpful.

Again, the problem has not been solved, but an "openness" has begun which provides an atmosphere in which the problem has the possibility of being worked through.

5. *Defining — Clarifying our own territory by making emotions known.*

> I STILL FEEL I HAVE A RIGHT TO KNOW AHEAD OF TIME IF I HAVE TO WORK LATE, SO THAT I CAN PLAN ON IT.

> WELL, WE CAN'T BOTHER ABOUT THAT NOW. YOU'LL HAVE TO STAY LATE, AND THAT'S IT.

He is so emotionally involved in getting something done, he isn't hearing him, and doesn't even acknowledge the fact that the request is a reasonable one.

6. *Defining — Protecting our own territory by quietly stating choices and taking appropriate action.*

> I KNOW HOW IMPORTANT THIS IS TO YOU, AND I'D LIKE TO HELP YOU, BUT I HAVE A VERY IMPORTANT APPOINTMENT MYSELF. . . . . . IF WE CAN WORK OUT SOME OTHER WAY OF DOING IT. I'LL DO WHAT I CAN. IF YOU INSIST ON MY STAYING LATE TONIGHT THOUGH, I FEEL SO STRONGLY ABOUT THIS THAT I WILL START LOOKING FOR ANOTHER JOB.

Informing the other of his plan of action is also a risking of the relationship.

> I GUESS WE BOTH FEEL VERY STRONGLY ABOUT THIS. I DON'T WANT YOU TO LEAVE, BUT ON THE OTHER HAND IF YOU DON'T STAY LATE AND HELP WITH THIS IT'S GOING TO CREATE A LOT OF PROBLEMS FOR ME.

> I KNOW YOU'RE ON THE SPOT AND I'D LIKE TO HELP, BUT IT'S REALLY VERY IMPORTANT FOR ME TO LEAVE ON TIME TONIGHT. I WISH I COULD HELP.

While nothing has been solved in regard to the problem, the openness that has occurred here has reached a point where practical solutions can be considered.

7. *Exploring Alternatives — Examining solutions with self respect.*

> I WONDER IF THIS COULD BE SOLVED IN SOME OTHER WAY.

> WHAT DO YOU HAVE IN MIND?

> NOTHING EXACTLY. IT JUST SEEMS THAT IT MIGHT HELP IF WE TOOK A SECOND LOOK AT THE PROBLEM.

227

ARE YOU SURE IT HAS TO BE FINISHED BY TEN O'CLOCK TOMORROW?

← "when must it be solved?"

YES. SMITH IS LEAVING HERE THEN AND HE HAS TO TAKE IT WITH HIM. HE HAS TO BE AT THE AIRPORT BEFORE NOON

MAYBE HE COULD TAKE PART OF IT NOW, AND GET THE REST LATER

An attempt to "expand the time availa

NO SUCH LUCK! HE JUST TOLD ME TODAY THAT HE HAS TO TAKE IT ALL WITH HIM.

SO EVERYTHING HAS TO BE COMPLETED BY TEN TOMORROW.

"The limits within which we must work"

COULD SOMEONE ELSE FLY OUT WITH IT LATER?

An attempt to change the limits, even though expensive.

NO. HE NEEDS IT WITH HIM.

228

I'D LIKE TO HELP, BUT....

LET'S THINK ABOUT THIS SOME MORE... LET'S SEE.... WHAT IS IT THAT WE ARE TRYING TO SOLVE?.... THIS IS DUE TOMORROW AT TEN AND YOU HAVE TO LEAVE..........

I WONDER IF WE'RE NOT MORE CONCERNED ABOUT A PARTICULAR SOLUTION THAN WHAT NEEDS TO BE DONE....

WHAT DO YOU MEAN?

WELL, WHEN YOU SAID "WHAT ARE WE TRYING TO SOLVE?" I REALIZED THAT THE REAL ISSUE IS NOT WHETHER I STAY LATE OR NOT, BUT GETTING THIS DONE BY TEN TOMORROW

AND......?

IF THE REAL PROBLEM IS GETTING THIS DONE BY TEN, I'D BE WILLING TO COME IN VERY EARLY TOMORROW MORNING AND FINISH IT THEN.

229

WOULD YOU?...THAT WOULD BE GREAT!...IF YOU'D BE WILLING TO DO THAT I'D SURE APPRECIATE IT!

I STILL FEEL STRONGLY ABOUT WHAT I SAID BEFORE THOUGH, ...THAT I HAVE A RIGHT TO KNOW AHEAD OF TIME IF I HAVE TO WORK LATE SO I CAN PLAN ON IT.

Even here there is some element of risk in defining territory again.

THAT'S FAIR...BUT I CAN'T ALWAYS PLAN AHEAD EITHER ...I SOMETIMES GET PRESSURED WHEN I DON'T EXPECT IT... AND THERE ARE EMERGENCIES THAT AREN'T ANYBODY'S FAULT. THEY JUST HAPPEN...

I'M WILLING TO WORK IN AN EMERGENCY...BUT YOU CAN UNDERSTAND HOW I FEEL.

YOU'LL HELP OUT IN A TOUGH SPOT, BUT YOU WANT ME TO KEEP YOU INFORMED.

YEAH.

O.K.

While other differences will arise after this incident future problems will be more easily solved because of this creative relationship.

230

COMMENTS ON THE PROCESS

1. How effective is this method of relating if only one person understands the process?

   One person can create a change in the relationship by being the first listener. Through listening, eventually a shift in attitude will occur in the other person. At that point the listener can request to be heard: "I've listened to you for a while, now will you feed back what you hear me saying? Then I'll listen to you again." If interruptions occur, listening again may be needed before repeating the above request.

2. Suppose, after each person has fully heard the other, there is still strong disagreement?

   Then, the person with the least amount of pain gives to the other. This is not the same as silently "giving in." It is an act of love based on the reality of the situation and concern for the other person. To measure the depth of the problem for each person is often difficult. Practically, it may be useful to ask each other, "On a scale of 1 to 10, how high is your pain in this situation?" If one person is continually feeling the most pain, it may be necessary to reevaluate the relationship itself. (See page 199.)

3. Doesn't defining and defending the territory create problems in a relationship?

Yes. That's usually the reason we avoid speaking up. Yet, remaining silent can cause underground resentment, which ultimately weakens the foundation of the relationship itself. (Resentment is equal to time we allow a person over our "ouch!" line without saying anything.) While expressing ourselves can cause temporary problems, it is a reality of life based on self worth, and so can't be disregarded. Problems created by speaking up can usually be resolved by alternately listening, each person clarifying for about five minutes before reversing that process.

We may hesitate to express small ouches ("It's so minor, it doesn't matter"). Yet, speaking up about them ("I'm somewhat bothered by . . .") will probably produce only minor responses. Small ouches continually held in, however, can build up and later cause a huge explosion.

Many difficulties in relationships could be avoided by each person agreeing on a basic rule: "I'll take responsibility for my 'ouch line.' If I don't speak up, you can assume all is well between us."

APPENDIX B

Comments on The Check List

CHECK LIST*

1. **What** specifically is to be solved?
2. **When** must it be solved?
3. Is it possible to **expand the time available** before a final decision must be made?
4. What are the **limits** within which we must work — those things that probably won't change? (Could any of these limits be changed though costly?)
5. Has the main **meaning** of the problem **for each person** been made clear?
6. Has holding on to a **particular solution** become more important than what needs to be done?
7. What **resources** are available to solve the problem?
8. Am I remaining open to a **new and unfamiliar solution** to the problem?
9. What is the **next step?**
10. Am I ue **emotions** to continually, test the solution being considered?

COMMENTS ON THE CHECK LIST

1. *What* specifically is to be solved?

Vagueness in defining the problem is often an obstacle in solving it.

The more specific we can be, the closer we are to an answer. (When a car stalls, if we can figure out *what* the problem is . . . [out of gas, battery dead, dirty carburetor, etc.], we have moved a long way toward solving the problem.)

Summarizing the problem in a sentence or two can sometimes be a key factor in moving toward a solution.

The more *specific* we can be, the closer we are to an answer.

I'D LIKE TO BE HAPPIER

is a vague statement, and not very helpful.

I'M UNHAPPY IN MY WORK BECAUSE
I HAVE ALMOST NO CONTACT WITH PEOPLE

is specific, and points the way toward a solution.

In moving toward an answer, after asking **what** is to be solved, it is also vital to ask:

2. **When** must it be solved?

Knowing when a final decision must be made has a great effect on **how** we go about solving the problem . . .

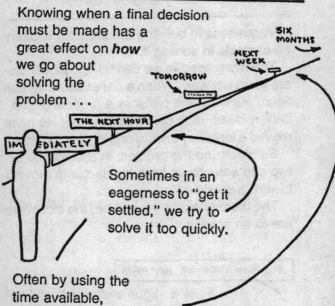

Sometimes in an eagerness to "get it settled," we try to solve it too quickly.

Often by using the time available, better solutions become possible, (more information may be available a new person may enter the situation, or the problem itself may change). Deciding **when** the problem **must** be solved may make us less anxious as well as mean a better decision.

238

Because time is so valuable in solving problems, it is also helpful to ask:

3. Is it possible to **expand the time available** before a final decision must be made?

While delaying a decision is sometimes simply avoiding responsibility, at other times time can be a valuable tool in making a better decision.

An immediate need may cause us to rush into a decision we may later regret.
Sometimes time can be expanded by using a temporary solution to meet the immediate need.
For example:
> It may be worth the expense to rent a car for a few days instead of buying one in haste simply because we need transportation.
> To buy a house in a new community on impulse because "school begins next week" may ultimately be far more costly than temporary lodging.

By examining the *reason* for the deadline we may find that the problem may be solved on a temporary basis and valuable time for further study can become available to us.

239

It is also useful to ask:

4. What are the *"limits"* within which we must work?

While constructive imagination can be hindered by deciding too quickly that "It won't work," ultimately we must face **the limits within which we must function**.

Sometimes problems do not get solved because too much time is spent in day-dreaming about what would happen if this or that were different instead of *facing those limits which probably will not change*.

An architect, in designing a building, is given certain limits within which he must work.

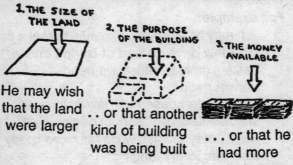

1. THE SIZE OF THE LAND

2. THE PURPOSE OF THE BUILDING

3. THE MONEY AVAILABLE

He may wish that the land were larger

.. or that another kind of building was being built

... or that he had more money

... but for practical purposes, his job is to **be as creative as possible within the limits he has been given.**

In every situation we are given certain limits which probably will not change in the near future, such as:

... dealing with a particular person daily.
... living within a limited income.
... living in a certain community.

... having experience in one kind of work.

... having physical limitations.

... living within certain organizational policies.

...etc.

— While it may be possible through effort and imagination, to ultimately change those limits, *in the meantime our task is to be* **as creative as possible within the limits we have been given today.**

In "clarifying the limits" we need to ask *what are those factors which probably will not change, within which we have to solve the problem?*

Some specific examples:

WHAT IS OUR MAXIMUM BUDGET FOR THIS?

ARE THERE ORGANIZATIONAL POLICIES WHICH LIMIT US? IF SO WHAT ARE THEY?

DOES LOCATION LIMIT US? IF SO, HOW?

IS HEALTH A FACTOR? IF SO, HOW?

ARE PERSONS LIMITING US? IF SO, IN WHAT WAY?

WHEN MUST THIS BE COMPLETED?

and, a very important question . . .

ARE THERE LIMITS WHICH COULD BE CHANGED, EVEN IF VERY EXPENSIVE? IS IT POSSIBLY WORTH THE EXPENSE?.

When two or more people are working on a problem, it becomes increasingly important to ask:

5. Has the main *meaning* of the problem *for each person* been made clear?

Every problem has many meanings. For example:

"a home power failure"
may mean

> I CAN'T SEE TO FINISH THIS WORK THAT'S DUE TOMORROW, AND I DON'T EVEN HAVE A FLASHLIGHT.

or

> I'M GETTING COLD BECAUSE THE FURNACE ISN'T WORKING.

or

> I'M GOING TO MISS MY FAVORITE TV SHOW.

While there are *many* meanings to a problem, some meanings are of more concern than others. It is important to discover the *central meaning* in any problem we face because, **the main meaning we give to a situation determines our actions.**

If the *main meaning* of "A HOME POWER FAILURE" is "**I can't see to work**" then our actions will focus on **"finding a temporary light."**

On the other hand, if the *main meaning* of "A HOME POWER FAILURE" is **"I'm getting cold,"** then the focus of our actions will be on *"a way to keep warm."*

While this may seem so obvious that it is hardly worth mentioning, in an actual relationship it may be far from obvious. *Assuming* that the other person "should know" what the problem means is a common cause of complications in a relationship.

> WHAT THE HELL ARE YOU DOING, JUST SITTING THERE? LOOK FOR A FLASHLIGHT!

or

> WHAT ARE YOU DOING UPSTAIRS? I'M FREEZING DOWN HERE, AND YOU DON'T EVEN CARE! YOU KNOW IT'S COLD!

It is vitally important for each person to make clear what the problem means to him.

> I'M WORRIED ABOUT HOW TO GET THAT WORK DONE FOR TOMORROW. I'M GOING TO LOOK FOR A FLASHLIGHT.

> I'M GLAD I'VE GOT THIS BLANKET NOW. I'M SO COLD I CAN'T MOVE!

244

6. Has holding on to a *particular solution*
   become more important than what needs to
   be done?

Often a power struggle is not over *what* is to be
done, but over *whose method* will be used.

Parents may, out of false pride, push for their
own way at the cost of what is best for the child.

Business associates, in an attempt to win a
point may destroy a common purpose.

Husband and wife, by each insisting on
certain roles for the other "for the sake of a
better relationship" may be preventing the very
happiness they both want.

When a struggle over method occurs it is often
best to put aside each person's solution, deal
with the emotions and begin again to explore
alternatives by asking "What, specifically, is
the problem?"

245

Sometimes, out of pride, we neglect to ask:

7. What *resources* are available to solve the problem?

Hours of time can be wasted, and work duplicated, by not making use of information that is readily available.

We might ask:

> IS THERE ANYONE WHO HAS SOLVED THIS PROBLEM, OR A SIMILAR ONE WHO COULD HELP?

> HOW COULD I GET INFORMATION ABOUT PEOPLE WHO MIGHT HELP?

> WHERE IS PRINTED MATERIAL AVAILABLE?

> ARE THERE RECORDS ON FILE THAT WOULD BE HELPFUL?

> IS THERE A PLACE I COULD VISIT WHERE A SIMILAR PROBLEM IS SOLVED?

When we face a problem for which there seems to be "no answer," one of the most useful things we can do is explore resources and gather information.

8. Am I remaining open to a *new and unfamiliar solution* to the problem?

Because experiences from our past greatly influence what we see and do not see, we tend to use those solutions which fit our pattern of thinking and neglect the unfamiliar.

To allow ourselves to really see something from another's viewpoint,

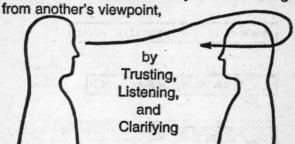

by
Trusting,
Listening,
and
Clarifying

We may open the way to a new, creative answer to a problem.

Unfortunately, the fear that the other person's viewpoint might *change us* or make us *feel like a child* may keep us from hearing.

yet, **TO BE WILLING TO HEAR ANOTHER'S VIEWPOINT, IS TO ACT CREATIVELY.**

To let go of the familiar is the way to creativity.

Questions encourage imagination:

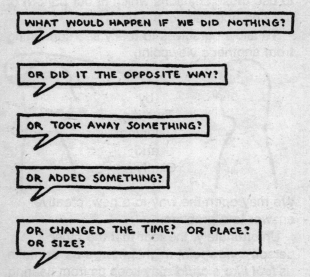

WHAT WOULD HAPPEN IF WE DID NOTHING?

OR DID IT THE OPPOSITE WAY?

OR TOOK AWAY SOMETHING?

OR ADDED SOMETHING?

OR CHANGED THE TIME? OR PLACE? OR SIZE?

Questions such as these may be explored with someone else or thought through individually for discussion later.

The questions will vary according to the specific problem. Almost every question is helpful if it causes us to see that which is familiar from a fresh perspective.

248

9. What is the *next step?*

Instead of waiting for "the final solution" before action is taken, it may be helpful, *if one step is clear to* **TAKE** *that one step*. The present solution does not have to be the final solution.

Most of us, in solving problems, want a searchlight available which will clearly show us the way, and our final destination . . .

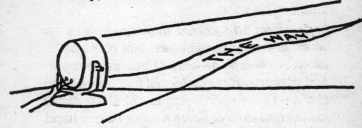

Yet, when we want a "final" answer immediately most problems become overwhelming to us:

> *"What career is best for me?"*
> *"How can I live with this person 30 more years?"*
> *"What will I do if I'm pregnant?"*
> *"How can I handle an alcoholic problem?"*

In reality, living is something like walking with
a flashlight in which all we can see is *the next step* . . .

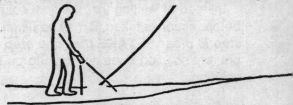

. . . *which is all we need to
see,* for once we have taken that one step, we
and the flashlight move forward and the next
step can be seen.

In deciding on a career there are small steps
which *are* clear possibilities, that could be
taken . . . finding an area of general interest
and talking with people about it . . . or reading
about it . . . or even trying to get a non-skilled
job in an area to observe a career close hand.

. . . once a step is taken, more light is
available for the *next* step.

*In deciding what to do about living with a
difficult person* there are steps that could be
taken . . . (Trusting, Listening and Clarifying is
a good beginning!) . . . another is seeking
counseling . . . or asking questions and
exploring possibilities — what would happen if
we separated? . . . Where would each go? . . .
What is available? . . . etc.

250

In exploring what to do about a problem pregnancy ... the first clear step might be to explore if the pregnancy exists ... if so, are there agencies available to help me? How and when could I find out more? ... Is there anyone I could talk with about it? When? ... etc.

... the point here is to ***begin*** solving the problem, by at least getting information, so that the best choice can ultimately be made.

In facing alcoholic problems, simple, quick, and easy solutions are seldom possible..To meet with those who have experience and practical suggestions, however, *is* possible. To visit a meeting of Alcoholics Anonymous, or a meeting of their Al-Anon, (to learn how to live with a problem drinker), is one way of beginning. Most phone books list Alcoholics Anonymous. A ***first step*** could be to ***dial the phone number and ask about it.***

Instead of waiting for "the final solution," if one step is ***clear***, we ***can*** take that one step.

10. Am I using my *emotions* to continually test the solution being considered?

While emotions can sometimes cloud the free exchange of information . . . if, when facts are being considered, we LISTEN to our emotions we can greatly enrich our understanding.

Emotions are a sensitive indicator that reaches into our being at a deeper level than logic.

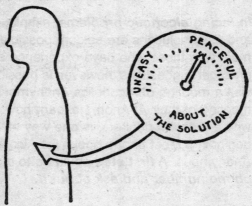

Listening for our own emotional responses, and the responses of others, provides a useful guide in making decisions.

252

Bibliography

Angyal, Andras, *Neurosis and Treatment*. John Wiley & Sons, Inc., New York, 1965.

Assagioli, Roberto, *The Act of Will*. The Viking Press, New York, 1973.

de Bono, Edward, *New Think*. Basic Books, Inc., New York, 1967.

Dobzhansky, Theodosius, *The Biology of Ultimate Concern*. The New American Library, New York, 1967.

Dreikus, Rudolf, and Grey, Loren, *Logical Consequences*. Meredith Press, New York, 1968.

Erikson, Erik H., *Childhood and Society*. W.W. Norton & Co. Inc., New York, 1950, 1963.

Fromm, Erich, *The Art of Loving*. Harper and Brothers, New York, 1956.

Ginott, Haim G., *Between Parent and Child*. Macmillan Co., New York, 1965.

Goble, Frank G., *The Third Force*, Grossman Publishers, New York, 1970.

Gordon, Thomas, *Parent Effectiveness Training*. Peter H. Wyden, New York, 1970.

Harris, Thomas, *I'm OK — You're OK*. Harper & Row, New York, 1967.

James, Muriel, and Jongeward, Dorothy, *Born To Win*. Addison-Wesley Publishing Co., Reading, Massachusetts, 1971.

Koestler, Arthur, *The Act of Creation*. Dell Publishing, New York, 1967.

Lair, Jess, *"I Ain't Much Baby — But I'm All I've Got."* Doubleday & Co., New York, 1972.

Land, George T. Lock, *Grow or Die*. Random House, New York, 1973.

Lederer, Wm. J., and Jackson, Don D., *The Mirages of Marriage*. W.W. Norton, New York, 1968.

Lowen, Alexander, *Pleasure: A Creative Approach To Life*. Coward-McCann, Inc., New York, 1970.

Luthman, Shirley Gehrke, *Itimacy: The Essence of Male and Female*. Nash Publishing, Los Angeles, 1972.

Mahrer, Alvin R., and Pearson, Leonard (Edited by), *Creative Developments In Psychotherapy Vol. 1*. The Press of Case, Western Reserve University, Cleveland, 1971.

Maslow, Abraham M., *Motivation and Personality*. Harper & Row, New York, 1954.

Maslow, Abraham M. (Edited by), *New Knowledge in Human Values*. Harper & Row, New York, 1970.

Maslow, Abraham M., *Toward a Psychology of Being*. D. Van Nostrand, Princeton, N.J., 1962.

May, Rollo, *Love and Will*. W.W. Norton, New York, 1969.

May, Rollo, *Power and Innocence*. W.W. Norton, New York, 1972.

May, Rollo (Edited by), *Existential Psychology*. Random House, New York, 1961.

Mayeroff, Milton, *On Caring*. Harper & Row, New York, 1971.

Misseldine, W. Hugh, *Your Inner Child of the Past*. Simon and Shuster, New York, 1963.

O'Neill, Nena and George, *Open Marriage*. M. Evans and Company, Inc., New York, 1972.

Parnes, Sidney J., and Harding, Harold F. (Edited by), *A Source Book for Creative Thinking*. Charles Scribner's Sons, New York, 1962.

Rogers, Carl R., *On Becoming a Person*. Houghton Mifflin Co., Boston, 1961.

Perls, Frederick S., Hefferline, R.F., Goodman, Paul, *Gestalt Therapy*. Julian Press, New York. 1951.

Perls, Frederick S., *Gestalt Therapy Verbatim*. Real People Press, Lafayette. California. 1969.

Polanyi, Michael, *Personal Knowledge*. University of Chicago Press, Chicago, 1958.

Prather, Hugh, *Notes To Myself*. Real People Press, Lafayette, California, 1970.

Shostrom, Everett L., *Man The Manipulator*. Abingdon Press, Nashville, 1967.

Tillich, Paul, *The Courage To Be*. Yale University Press, New Haven, 1952.

Uris, Auren, *The Executive Deskbook*. Van Nostrand Reinhold Company, New York, 1970.

Van Dusen, Wilson, *The Natural Depth in Man*. Harper & Row, New York, 1972.

Williams, Roger J., *You Are Extraordinary*. Random House, New York, 1967.